*POULTRY FANCIERS LIBRARY*

# MANAGING POULTRY
## for
# EXHIBITION

# OTHER BOOKS AVAILABLE

# MANAGING POULTRY
## for
## EXHIBITION

## H Easom Smith

*Past President : Poultry Club*

## Revised by Joseph Batty

*Past President : Old English Game Club*

**Beech Publishing House**
The Bindery
Sawmill Buildings
Stedham, Midhurst,
West Sussex GU29 ONY

First published 1974
This impression 1994

ISBN   1-85259-017-3

**Beech Publishing House**
The Bindery
Sawmill Buildings
Stedham, Midhurst,
West Sussex   GU29   ONY

# CONTENTS

# ILLUSTRATIONS

# EDITORS' FOREWORD

*Managing Poultry for Exhibition* represents the author's experience of a lifetime in which poultry has played a dominant part.

Keeping poultry, ensuring that they comply with the Poultry Standards, and showing them at their best, all require considerable knowledge and skill. Mr. H. Easom Smith has brought together in this volume hints, notes and sound advice; whether the reader is a beginner or an established fancier he is likely to gain from studying what has been written.

We feel sure that readers will welcome this book to the Series just as much as we have.

J. Batty

# PREFACE

THIS BOOK has been written only for those who love their poultry. It is intended to fall into the hands of people who take pride in the health of their fowls; who admire them for their fine form, their colour, their adornments and their condition. But, chiefly, for their high condition which enables the cocks to strut with more pride than many other birds and their hens to fulfil the instincts with which Nature endowed them, especially the maternal instinct.

Should the pages which follow be scanned by someone who thinks that poultry are merely a factor in the equation:
Genetic potential + Controlled environment + Balanced feeding = More eggs + More flesh + More profit
then I would respectfully ask them to gain pleasure from the pursuit of the ideal fowl in the highest condition or stop reading and go back to the stresses which surround their chosen form of poultry-keeping.

My age is such that I have been enabled to know some of the pioneers of Standard poultry — men who actually made first importations of leading breeds like Wyandottes, Plymouth Rocks and Leghorns from their countries of origin. Looking back over more than fifty years of interest in show poultry I recall names of many who are now truly regarded as "great" breeders and exhibitors.

In my younger days I always enjoyed visiting and talking to successful fanciers. Many of them passed on the odd hint which proved useful. Some of them would talk and then ask me not to write about the matter under discussion. Others were as generous as the day was long and freely placed their knowledge at my disposal. Somewhere in this book is the essence of anything I learned from them as well as what my own experience taught me. This includes classic wins as far back as the 1920s and judging at many shows, among them the Crystal Palace in its heyday — just before it was burned down.

The cult of gallinaceous birds came strongly to the fore when Victoria was a young queen. It was then that astute breeders realised that domestic fowls of better form and colour were worth more than the usual sorts. The first big step forward was in segregating and producing such birds.

With the establishment of shows on orderly lines, the second step to success was taken by people who studied management so that their birds were usually better presented than those of their rivals.

Finally, the peak position in the world of show poultry was gained by those whose method of grooming and showmanship enabled their fine birds to look finer still. These fanciers did the poultry fancy a great service by setting up new standards towards which others could strive. In time, the general level of presentation improved.

Among the more flamboyant showmen, the egoist and egotist came to the fore; the very nature of competition encourages these traits of human nature. Such people could find very little they would want to know in this book. They had already subscribed to the doctrine that all knowledge consists in the ideas of one's own mind and claimed (maybe, through trial and error) to have come up with all the right answers.

I make no such claim. What I give is a guide to many facets of management of show poultry which are sure to present a few problems during a fancier's career. It has always been my experience that someone, somewhere, at some time, had found a solution which he was ready to pass on: and I hope I have passed it on, too.

I have tried to avoid just setting down a gallimaufry of methods and striven to give coherent and reasoned chapters based on "tried and true" ways by which fowls may be got fit; well conditioned; well shown and altogether prize-worthy, in the hope they will be helpful to all those who seek advice on this fascinating and delightful aspect of the domestic fowl.

H. EASOM SMITH

Gatherley Castle,
Brompton on Swale.

# PREFACE TO SECOND EDITION

Additions have been made in a number of places in the pages which follow and sketches, illustrating some of the points made in the text, have been added. It is gratifying to know that there is a continued need for a guide to show poultry of the kind still offered and that this pleasant aspect of poultry keeping continues to have a firm following.

Sedlescombe,
East Sussex. H. Easom Smith.

# PREFACE TO THIRD EDITION

Sadly H. Easom Smith is no longer able to keep this book up-to-date and I have attempted to step into the breach. Interest in poultry showing continues to grow and it is hoped that this book will continue to serve fanciers for many more years.

J. Batty

*Frontispiece:* Points of the Fowl

# CHAPTER 1

## HAVE AN OBJECTIVE

### ESSENTIAL REQUIREMENTS

ANY FOWL CAN be managed so that it becomes physically fit enough to be conditioned for show. But this does not necessarily make it prizeworthy. All the good management on earth cannot make a bird any better than it already is in Standard points.

The chapters which follow set out in reasonably logical order various steps necessary to breed and condition poultry so that they may finally appear before the judges in all their glory and with a very good chance of winning prizes.

But the whole exercise must turn on the excellence of fowls themselves; if deficient in Standard points no amount of effort will cause them to seem to be of such quality that judges cannot pass them by.

The first thing the prospective exhibitor must determine — and only he can do this — is what he would like to achieve.

Poultry exhibitors seem to me to fall into three well defined categories. These are:

1. **Leading exhibitors**, with a reputation as winners.
2. **Breeder/exhibitors**, who breed all their own exhibits.
3. **Suppliers of foundation stock**, who only exhibit as a means of advertising.

### LEADING EXHIBITORS

To these people, whose support of shows is often on a massive scale, there is no pleasure to equal that of having their names engraved on the top trophies at the leading shows. They do not always breed their own winners; are, in fact, often content merely to own the best specimens in their chosen breeds, regardless of where they were originally bred.

One does not decry their efforts, since their showing is generous and their entries thankfully received by show promoters, but buying from several different sources cannot result in the consistent breeding of winners from winners and they may have to return to the open market often and dearly.

Prices will rise to them as their reputations grow but the young stock they produce will not necessarily be of much use to the person just setting out to breed show stock. The reason for this is that their breeding stock will derive from several different sources. Young stock, bred from such a pen, will not necessarily closely resemble their parents. They will be heterozygous and may even, in some cases, revert to some undesirable traits which their ancestors showed. In any case, they cannot exhibit enough close family likeness to be wholly desirable by new breeders.

Although it may be completely true that all the parent stock, in the breeding pen, have won many awards at shows it is beyond the power of anyone to guarantee that offspring from birds bought in from several different places will produce youngsters of equal merit.

## BREEDER/EXHIBITORS

Many prefer to be known as breeder/exhibitors. That is, their chief happiness comes from having bred the birds they show and they will never willingly buy a bird merely to have it for showing.

Occasionally, these people have to buy a bird for stock purposes and give it just one outing to measure it against others of its kind. By and large, they prefer to mate their pens so that they will breed winners: to hatch and rear their chicks so that they are satisfying as growers: to mature and condition their young adults so that they are a credit to them in the exhibition pen: to nurse their mature stock through the moult and present them as prizeworthy oldsters: to support all the shows they can and get as many awards as their stock merits at the leading shows of the year.

These breeder/exhibitors are people of much merit but, especially when one-breed specialists, they are often bigoted in their appreciation of other exhibits.

## FOUNDATION STOCK BREEDERS

The third group of exhibitors pick and choose their shows with care. They do not usually give generous support at a full

2

circuit of shows, but put their specimens on view only at those events which offer major prizes, e.g. their annual club shows and the classics, where there is most likely to be a good number of prospective buyers.

These are leading breeders showing to make and maintain a name as persons with stock of highest merit from whom sound breeding and show birds can usually be bought.

Some of them are dictatorial; some are "dog in the manger-ish" when it comes to the crunch of parting with some of their better class birds; some are open-handed and generous to the extreme. All of them will be able to provide that sort of start with a breeding pen which might put a beginner right to the top in the minimum time.

Even so, the new breeder will be well advised to visit the person from whom he wishes to buy stock and keep his eyes open all the time. Does there appear to be a common fault running through all the members of the stud, which is accentuated in those birds which their owner left at home as compared with those he exhibited? Is there a tendency to oversize in bantams or undersize in large fowls and is the breeder limited in his choice to those few which approximate to the norm, for the breed? Does the stud contain a reasonable proportion of adult stock or has it tendency to produce "flat-catchers" which last only for one season?

These and allied questions can be answered by the observant buyer without ever voicing a query — merely by acute observation. And he should know, at the end of his visit, whether this is really the breeder from whom he wishes to buy foundation stock. Or whether he must seek elsewhere.

There may be a fourth group of people in this world of show poultry but their efforts are so woefully inconsistent and their exhibits encompass so many odd specimens of different breeds that I may be forgiven if I regard them as the weaker brethren of my first group of top exhibitors. But they have this great merit — they are "hanging about" doing odd jobs at poultry exhibitions.

The targets of different exhibitors vary, as indicated. It follows that expenditure on basic stock and that needed to continue successfully in the poultry fancy will also differ.

A skilful breeder/exhibitor may be able to make ends meet over a full season of showing. He could, if prepared to sell a few birds for stock and show, make a profit at the year end.

The leading breeder, with his more economical approach to showing, looks to make a profit by the sale of stock and hatching eggs. The ardent showman, buying here and there, can only look to his list of cup and special prize wins to make his balance sheet look rosy.

## ALL HAVE COMMON OBJECTIVE

All of them have this one thing in common, though. They must study their birds, especially the specimens destined for exhibition, and treat them as individuals.

No two birds are alike in their habits, even if hatched and reared together from the same identical parents. As they have grown, a natural pecking order has been established and those with robust manners (even as far as being absolute bullies) have become apparent. In the same way, the timid bird has been discovered. In between, the normally happy mob seems to thrive under most conditions, although they do vary, bird by bird.

## THEIR BIRDS VARY

One may eat a lot of greenfood and not scratch vigorously for corn. Another may tend to stand about and pack up with easily eaten soft mash, when it is given. A third may come into lay early and soon show signs of losing condition in plumage by constant visits to the nest box, while another may lay smaller eggs and keep her bodily condition very well.

These are suggestions of pointers to look for. They can only be found by steady observation at all times. When seen, they should be memorised because, when birds are being put up for individual treatment, peculiar traits become doubly important.

For greatest success, therefore, do not think of show poultry as a flock or even as easily managed units in small houses. Think of them as individuals and treat them so that Nature is helped and not hindered when conditioning for exhibition takes place.

## SUMMARY

As indicated, there are different types of exhibitors all of whom are striving to present first class stock. For consistent success at shows, birds kept must have as many points of excellence as possible. In addition, each should be treated as an individual and in conditioning him (or her) every effort should be made to magnify virtues and to reduce the effects of any weaknesses.

Figure 1. A Large Brown Red Old English Game Cock

# CHAPTER 2

## SUITABLE HOUSING SYSTEMS

### BREED INFLUENCES HOUSING

EXHIBITION POULTRY are usually kept in relatively small numbers. In those rare instances where farm accommodation is at the fancier's disposal, with almost unlimited space for poultry, pre-planning is not as essential as when space is limited.

In the majority of cases it is very necessary for the poultry-man to assess his precise requirements before he starts to create a layout of houses and runs.

To help him in this matter he should take into account not only size but the nature of his fowls as well. He could succeed with sedate and stately Orpingtons in smaller runs than with extremely active Anconas, for instance. He could build one large unit and divide it up for Pekin bantams, but not for Old English Game bantams.

Some idea of what he wishes to accommodate, both in nature and in numbers, will be the guide and best results got from a housing system which is tailored to requirements.

**Example**

Minimum requirements for the one-breed specialist who wishes to breed his own exhibition stock are:

Two Breeding Pens.

Two pens for growing cockerels.

Two pens for growing pullets.

Additionally, provision should be made for hatching and rearing, preferably on rested ground each year, and not on the main site more or less permanently occupied by adults.

Precise needs for rearing are not discussed here since our theme is management for exhibition which starts with the "growing" stages.

### SUITABLE SYSTEMS

The most suitable systems have proved themselves to be:
1. Large houses with interior divisions, on a permanent site.

2. Series of small houses, with outdoor runs, on a permanent site.
3. Movable units on a large, lawn area.
4. Strawyard, under farmstead conditions.

These are considered in that order.

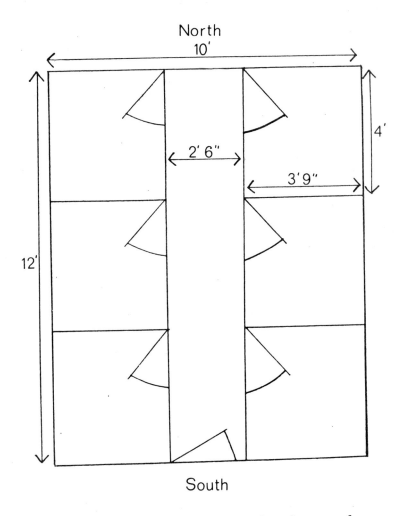

Figure 2.  Plan to provide six units under one roof.

## LARGE, PERMANENT HOUSE

This system is used with great success by people whose back gardens are of relatively small size and whose main interest is in bantams.

The house is built with a span roof so that there is maximum headroom for the fancier down the middle of the house.

Suppose the area of the house to be 12ft. by 10ft., its walls 5 ft. high and the ridge 6 ft. 6 in. It is sited so that the solid end is to the north, the door end is to the south and the other walls lie east and west. This gives maximum resistance to winter weather which is likely to come from the north and maximum daylight through the windows which face east (for early morning sun) and west (for afternoon sunshine). The attendant's door, in the south end, can be left open as required to admit more sunshine, should this be thought necessary.

A central aisle, 2 ft. 6 in. wide, is for the convenience of the attendant. Interior divisions are all 3 ft. 9 in. wide by 4 ft. long, following the division of the house into six sections.

Partitions have solid divisions 1 ft. 6 in. high and then wire netting to roof level. The central aisle has similar construction except that each division has a door so that the attendant can pass into it as needful.

Ventilation to admit outflow of foul air or excess heat is through a gap along the ridge, which is covered by a cap to prevent rain driving in. The principle is that of the once-popular "Lancashire cabin" which housed thousands of commercial layers in other days.

When birds are kept in such a unit it is essential to maintain utmost cleanliness and have a rotation of thorough cleansing which is scrupulously maintained.

This is a sort of mini-outfit but it is large enough to enable a self-contained stud to be kept. The dimensions can, of course, be increased to accommodate more bantams or large fowl, as the fancy dictates. But the basic plan remains. See Figure 1 for details of layout.

## SMALL HOUSES, ON PERMANENT SITE

The plan, Figure 2, shows how a larger piece of garden or

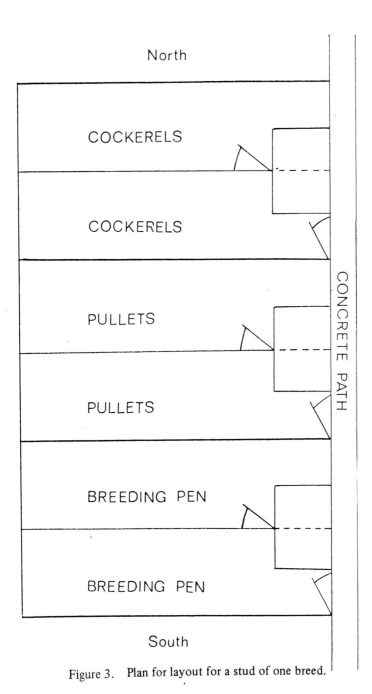

Figure 3. Plan for layout for a stud of one breed.

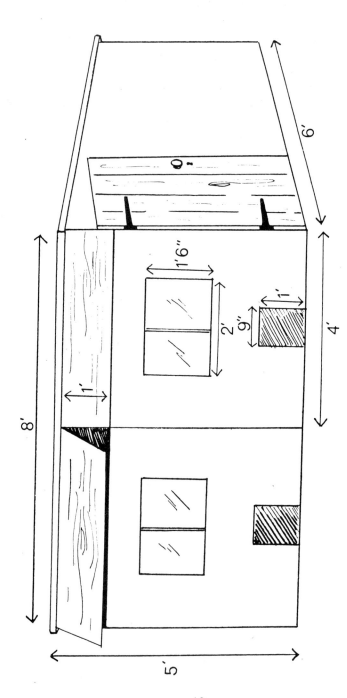

Figure 4.    Sketch of suitable all-purpose house.

10

orchard could be utilised to maintain a stud of any one breed. It envisages the provision of three houses, each of which is divided into two sections. There are six outdoor runs and the houses are so located that half of each of them serves one outdoor run.

It is necessary to choose the site for this outfit with care, in relation to the dwelling house. Access to each house will vary over the year. The two breeding pens will always be visited; the two pullet houses will not need a visit in late winter and early spring when their former inmates have been drafted into breeding pens and surplus sold. Two pens for cockerels will have lesser occupation, since most of them will be for disposal and all cleared out by the time the first breeding pen is put together, after the main shows are over.

A good path is needed, running the length of the combined units. By having one, the fancier can walk along as often as he likes, in any weather, and still not be tramping through mud. Concrete is cleanest and most durable and its uses are dealt with in Chapter 3.

The size and character of the chosen breed must again be taken into account before the plan is committed to paper, and certainly before any work is put in hand.

A suitable size for the cockerel and pullet houses (large breeds) is 8 ft. long by 6 ft. deep. Divided centrally, back to front, this gives two sections each 6 ft. by 4 ft.

For preference, each house should have a solid floor and be set up on piles so that the space underneath is available for shelter and as a dust bath.

The two cockerel houses should be equipped with perches and dropping boards but no nestboxes. Those for the pullets are similar but have nestboxes in them. The whole of the front should be devoted to ventilators, shutters, windows and pop-holes, the attendant's door being placed in each end of the houses (see Figure 3).

The outdoor runs should be reasonably large and there should be enough room for a gate, leading to and from the path. This gate should be wide enough for a garden barrow to pass through; a great facility when cleaning out thoroughly.

## MOVABLE UNITS ON LAWN

There are two sorts of movable units commonly in use.

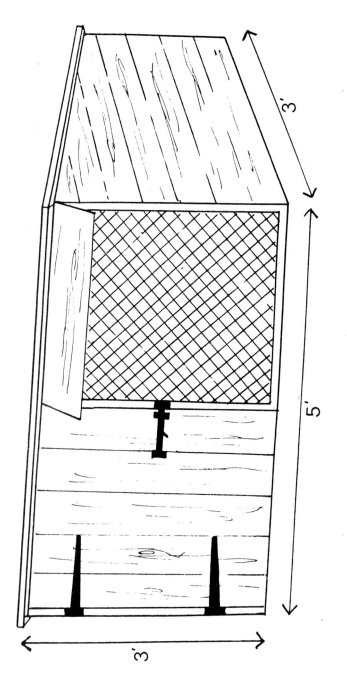

Figure 5. Sketch of simple portable unit.

One consists of a very simple, lean-to shelter as shown in Figure 4. The small door opens to a compartment which contains nestboxes in the breeding season and is fitted with a perch. The other section is under the same roof but only has a wire netted front and weather-board. The fowls drop their excrement on to the grass which the unit covers. The small area soon becomes fouled and it is vital to the success of this system that each unit is moved on to a clean area at frequent intervals. Ideally, each soiled area should be allowed a month's rest before another unit is placed on it. This means that a space, fourteen times the area of the total size of all the units, must be available; supposing each unit stays on each site for two days.

This system may attract some people who like their birds to live the "simple life" but is not conducive to as close control of exhibition stock as one would like and has, in my experience, mostly been used by fanciers of those old established true bantams, which breed best when warmer days are with us.

Rather better, but still not the most comfortable form of housing there is, I would rate the "Sussex" ark, of standard pattern. If these arks are to be large enough for the accommodation of heavy breeds they become cumbersome and must be fitted with a pair of wheels at one end and lifting handles at the other, in order to move them readily.

I have seen several of these units in use for fowls destined to lay eggs and provide chicken meat for a convalescent home, and the gardener-handyman whose job it was to look after the poultry had good success. But the laying of eggs is one thing; the preservation of show plumage is another altogether and I would prefer the permanent site to the portable unit or ark.

## STRAWYARDS

Should the fancier be fortunate enough to have a range of farm buildings, including loose boxes and fold-yards, he needs very little instruction as to how to get and keep his birds in grand condition.

The essence of the operation is to fit out a loose box or two with perches, nest boxes, ventilation, windows, etc., in such a way that they are snug enough for poultry, and to have access from them to a section of a fold-yard which has been copiously littered down with straw.

The birds revel in the conditions but it must not be thought that they will find their living, even though they remain actively scratching amongst the straw. Exhibition poultry need exhibition-type attention and feeding. Neither should be neglected because the birds are in such good surroundings. As the straw becomes broken up and the level sinks, more should be added. Final clearance is after the moult when the litter has become soiled and is full of old feathers.

## ESSENTIAL POINTS IN POULTRY HOUSES

All poultry houses, although their designs vary according to owners' wishes, must have certain things in common.
1. Weatherproof roof.
2. Draught-free walls.
3. Vermin-proof floor.
4. Adequate ventilation.
5. Adequate natural light.
6. Perches.
7. Droppings boards.
8. Pophole.
9. Attendant's door.
For houses of the size envisaged it is not necessary to cover the roof with corrugated sheets or tiles unless, by chance, the fancier can acquire these items at a very reduced price.

A weatherproof roof can be had by covering boards with roofing felt. This is chiefly based on bitumen and will repel rain, sleet and snow quite adequately, if only it is properly laid. If it is simply taken from the roll in which it is bought, laid on the boards and nailed down, it will wrinkle and bulge as soon as it is subjected to weather. Afterwards the wrinkles will crack and let rain in.

Before roofing a poultry shed, wait until a reasonably dry and warmish day comes along. Measure the length, side to side, of the roof and add 6 inches. Cut a strip to this length and lay it on the ground, placing bricks or other weights at the corners and along the edges to prevent wind damage. When the felt is pliable place the strip along the bottom of the roof, allowing 3 inches overlap at each end and along the bottom edge. Fix with suitable flat-headed nails along both edges only. Cut another similar strip, lay it out until ready, then place it so that it overlaps the first strip by about 3 inches. Nail along the top edge. Continue in this way until the roof is covered.

Now, nail on laths so that the felt is held down without being peppered with flat-headed nails, placing the laths 3 to 4 feet apart, according to size of the roof and running top to bottom. The bottom areas between the laths should be secured by triangular pieces of wood. The 3-inch overlaps all round the edge of the roof should be turned under and nailed.

Draught-free walls mean that any knotholes in timber, broken corners of asbestos sheeting and odd cracks in other material are suitably stopped by the use of putty, mastic or whatever suits the material.

To be vermin-proof the floor of a poultry house should be solid. If this cannot be contrived, and rammed earth is to be utilised, then steps should be taken to make it sound against incursions by rats or other burrowing animals. The top 6 inches of earth should be dug out and half-inch mesh wire netting laid down flat over the whole area of the floor, being turned up all round and nailed to the bottom edge of each wall. Next lay household ashes on the wire (centrally-heated home owners will utilise sharp gravel or something similar) and cover with about an inch of soil. The whole is then rammed down hard. More ashes and the rest of the earth are next spread over the floor and hard ramming takes place. Within reason, such action will keep out rats.

Ventilation, in small houses, comes from a space, covered with wire netting, which has a shutter which is hinged to close the aperture or which slides up and down within grooves. For a really small house a shutter, hinged at the top and covering a space along the whole of the front may be a little too much. It should, therefore, be reduced in length.

Adequate natural light follows the provision of suitable windows. With other means of ventilation these can be fixed permanently so that they are draughtproof. There is no limit to shape and size of windows with the one proviso that if most of the front of a house consists of glass and the birds are wanted for show, steps will have to be taken to shade the house fronts in high summer. This is necessary for two reasons; (a) to diffuse direct sunlight, especially for birds of delicate colouring like buffs, wheatens and blues and (b) to reduce heat caused by sun "drawing" on plain glass. Although some slight reduction in temperature may be gained by treating windows with whitewash it is better to fix **exterior** curtains or blinds which can be lowered or raised at will. If shades are fixed inside the windows there will certainly be a diminution of glare from the sun but no reduction of temperature.

Perches need be nothing more elaborate than a piece of batten with the corners planed off. I do not subscribe to the theory that a natural branch, cut from a tree, is best for the birds. There are too many knots and snags and there is varying thickness on most branches. Constant roosting on a static branch with protruding knots will cause damage to breastbones which may not be sustained by the same birds on the same branches swaying naturally outdoors – conditions which we can only contemplate for some Game fowl.

A droppings board is a fixed shelf, beneath perches, on to which fowls can void excrement while they roost. It should be scraped clean and the manure taken away each day.

The pophole may vary in size, breed by breed. A big combed Leghorn wants more head room to prevent damage to his comb than the larger bodied, but neat-headed, Wyandotte. Cut the hole, therefore, according to the breed, but ensure that it can be safely fastened up each night to prevent losses from predators.

# CHAPTER 3

## USES FOR CONCRETE

### PLANNING A PERMANENT LAYOUT

IN VIEW OF today's shortages of building materials and their prices, some thought should be given to using concrete to assist in making a better layout. This is particularly the case where prize poultry are to be kept in a back garden where the fancier must be careful not to cause offence to his neighbours in the pursuit of his hobby.

He should be concerned to have not only a neat and comprehensive layout, as suggested in the previous chapter, but also to see that the paths and surrounds to his runs are capable of being kept clean and weedfree.

Concrete paths are durable and clean, allowing the poultryman to reach fowl houses in comparative comfort in any weather. For best results the concrete should be made to a reasonably exact formula and the paths be properly laid.

Although pre-cast concrete slabs make a very good path they involve the tedious business of laying them on a firm and level bed. Ready-mixed concrete can be had in most localities and while it cuts out the handmixing of dry ingredients and blending them into concrete it has the drawback of being delivered in one enormous heap which must be laid while it is still in workable condition.

Taking all things together my advice is that the poultryman who desires concrete paths to his exact liking should buy the materials in relatively small lots and make his own concrete.

It should be noted that the building trade now deals in metric measures and material will need to be bought on that basis. The information which follows has been provided by one of my sons who is professionally a member of the management team of one of the leading manufacturers of concrete products.

### MATERIALS

Cement, sand, stones and water are the constituent parts of concrete. The sand must be "sharp" as opposed to "soft" builders' sand which is used only for making mortar. The stones are often referred to as "coarse aggregate" and can either be gravel or crushed stone not larger than about 20 mm. (¾ in.) nor smaller than 5 mm. ($\frac{3}{16}$ in.). Cement is the standard greyish Portland cement as sold by builders' merchants and is usually packed in 50 kg. bags.

## Formula

1 part cement
2 parts sharp sand
3 parts aggregate, all parts by volume
Water.

## Tools required

Shovel
Buckets of the same size
Watering can with rose affixed
Rake
Float (made of a piece of wood, for levelling)
Hose pipe affixed to water supply or outside tap
Timber for forming straight edges
Hammer and nails.

## Amount required

Measure out the length of the path and decide how wide it should be. Decide how thick the concrete should be in relation to the amount of wear and tear it is likely to get and what weight it will be required to bear at any one time. 75 mm. (3 in.) is recommended as likeliest to suit all normal needs. Multiply the length of the path by the width to give an area in square metres. Now multiply this figure by the desired thickness of the path expressed as a fraction of a metre. This will give the amount in cubic metres ($m^3$) of concrete needed.

### Example

For a path 20 metres long and 1 metre wide, there would be a surface area of 20 square metres ($m^2$). For a thickness of 75 mm. or .075 metres the number of cubic metres of concrete required would be 1.5 ($m^3$).

Thus:

Length x width x thickness (in fractions of metre) = cubic metres.

## Quantities

The quantities for 1 m³ of concrete, to the formula given are:

| | |
|---|---|
| 7 bags of cement | or, if an all-in |
| .50 m³ of sharp sand | aggregate base is |
| .75 m³ of coarse aggregate. | bought 1.00 m³. |

## METHOD FOR AN *IN SITU* CONCRETE PATH

If the recommended thickness of 75 mm. is adopted, then surface material should be removed to this depth below the desired final level of the path. The site should be as level as possible and the excavated area filled with "hard core". This can consist of broken bricks, stone or similar durable, hard material. It should be broken evenly and rammed or rolled to compact it.

Lengths of wood, of a depth suitable to create the 75 mm. concrete path, should be set on edge along both sides of the prepared area. A garden line or similar device should be used to get straight edges and regular width. The wooden "shuttering" should have stout pegs driven against it on the outside of the path to prevent the boards bulging outwards when the weight of concrete is laid within the boundary created.

Since concrete expands and contracts with changes of temperature it should be laid in bays not exceeding 2.5 m. (8 ft.) long. Thin, softwood laths are laid across the path at this suitable distance and left *in situ*.

If the ground is dry when path laying takes place, it should be damped before placing the concrete and the mixed concrete should be laid within one hour of mixing. Spread the concrete with a shovel, work it well into place using the edge of the shovel and rake it down to a height of about 6 mm. (¼ in.) above the side shuttering. The concrete should be compacted by working a length of stout board, with a good straight edge, over the surface. If it is first "chopped" down then sawed backwards and forwards it will be found that the material goes down evenly. A non-slip surface, which is of great advantage in frosty winter conditions, can be achieved by brushing over the surface after the material has been laid for about one hour.

Newly-laid concrete should be covered with polythene sheet or dampened sacking for two or three days after laying so that it does not dry out too violently, on the one hand, or receive a large amount of rain, on the other.

**How to make hand-mixed concrete**

There should be a clean, hard surface (such as another area of concrete) or a platform of hardboard or similar material. There should be enough "elbow room" and the poultryman should not try to make his wet mix in the midst of his three lots of dry ingredients or he will be courting trouble by prematurely wetting some of his residual material and getting his mix unbalanced by "dragging in" sand and aggregate he should not have.

For measuring the materials in bulk, use one dry bucket of reasonably small size for cement, fill it up each time and "strike it off" level with a piece of board. Use an exactly similar bucket for sand and aggregate so that all measures are equal.

For the suggested mix take 1 bucket of cement, 2 of sand and 3 of aggregate and have about ¾ bucket of water ready.

Form a flat, circular layer of aggregate then add the sand. Add the cement and mix dry, turning it over twice. Form a crater and add half the water. Throw the material from the outside edges to the top and mix. This will be too dry but consistency is gained by adding water from a watering can fitted with a rose so that all the heap can be evenly wetted. Chop the heap with a shovel, keep turning it edges to middle and pat it down with the shovel until the whole mass is evenly moist but not soggy wet. Turn again and if "cement" can be brought to the top by simply patting with the back of the shovel, the concrete is ready for laying.

The mixing area should be swept and hosed down as soon as possible after use. All tools should be hosed down until no traces of concrete remain on them, even if they are to be used for another mix later the same day. For ease of work, it is critical to have a clean site and clean tools on each occasion.

## MAKING SLABS AND POSTS

The formula given will make a concrete to produce slabs, posts, etc., for use in the poultry pens. It is necessary to make a wooden mould with precise interior dimensions and to ensure that the concrete has no air pockets in it when moulds are filled to create whatever is wanted. This is achieved by patient tamping down with a rammer or rod and by filling the mould gradually and not all at one time. Moulds must be treated with oil to ease de-moulding when the concrete is set.

When slabs are wanted to go round run bottoms or posts to support wire netting they should be designed so that wooden plugs are inserted in the wet concrete where fixing holes are required. These are easily drilled out when the product is dry. Such pre-cast jobs should have their moulds removed after two days and be left to "cure" for about seven days in good weather before they are used.

## CONCRETE BUILDINGS

These are beyond the scope of the average home concreter but can be bought ready-made from several manufacturers. They do, of course, provide absolutely vermin-proof shelter for the stock and are extremely durable. My own experience with small livestock suggests that they should be lined with some warmer material, e.g., thin timber, plasterboard, chipboard and so on and there should be a vapour-proof barrier between the inside of the concrete wall and the inner lining. This can be achieved by a good coat of aluminium paint on the interior face of the lining; i.e., that face which is normally seen inside the house.

Except for something like a food store or a really excellent penning house this would be thought too elaborate by the average poultry breeder and would hardly justify its cost.

# CHAPTER 4

## FURTHER ACCOMMODATION TO AID PRIZEWINNING

### ANCILLARY NEEDS

In addition to main layout of houses, already described, some ancillary equipment is needed if birds are to be presented at shows in the best possible condition. Essentials are:

1. Penning room.
2. Range of small houses for individual birds.
3. Food store.
4. Exhibition hampers.
5. Broody breaker.

It is optional whether a hospital pen be provided or whether one of the small houses be set apart and used only as a sick bay.

### PENNING ROOM

The pens in general use at shows up and down the country are about 2 ft. 3 in. cube for large fowl and 1 ft. 6 in. cube for bantams. It is necessary to train exhibition poultry so that they adapt themselves readily to such confinement, keeping well "on show" and not crouching away in a corner, because of the close proximity of onlookers.

The size of a penning room will depend on the number and size of the birds to be conditioned for show. With the pen dimensions already given it is easy to work out what's wanted in each case.

### Method

It is better to build pens with solid sides, backs and tops and only have the regulation wire fronts. If complete sets of pens are bought the tops and backs will consist of wire bars and some additional benching will have to be constructed to support them.

Regulation show hampers — again pay regard to the size of the breed — will have one, two, three or four compartments. Their dimensions of length will vary but height and width will be constant. Each owner will know what size baskets he needs to store between shows.

22

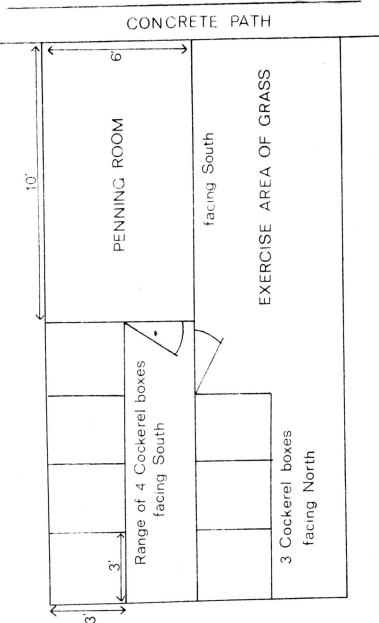

Figure 6. Plan of area for penning house and ancillary equipment for final conditioning.

23

With a solid floor beneath his feet the fancier should measure the height of his exhibition hampers and then arrange a wooden shelf at such a height that the baskets will slide under it.

The shelf will be the full length of the house and either 2 ft. 3 in. from the back wall for large fowls or 1 ft. 6 in. for bantams.

A second shelf, of the same size, is built either 2 ft. 3 in. or 1 ft. 6 in. above the first one. Divisions are now constructed between the two shelves at such intervals that each takes a wire front, equipped with sliding door. The divisions should be capable of removal so that, when a trio is being matched and schooled it may have the benefit of a double-sized pen.

A similar set of pens is arranged on the upper shelf and provided with a solid top.

Height of the back wall of the house is determined by the combined height of show baskets plus two rows of pens.

In Figure 5 the penning house is shown measuring 10 ft. by 6 ft. This is not an arbitrary figure but the bare minimum for comfort of both the birds and their owner. It would be better if larger in all directions.

The penning room should have a span roof to give head-room to the attendant and ventilation is best derived from hopper windows and ridge aperture. Even though facing south to gain maximum sunshine in the worst parts of the year, a penning room ventilated in this way would not be unreasonably stuffy in the height of summer if curtains were provided over the windows to shade them.

The purpose for which a penning room is first provided should remain the paramount reason for its existence. It should not become a place where sick and ailing birds are constantly being tended nor a spot where broody hens are sitting on their eggs.

Temptation to have some of the choicer birds, not destined for the breeding pen, living permanently in showpens should be resisted. They will do best if kept in an outdoor house and only brought in after washing or for final conditioning and titivating.

## RANGE OF SMALL HOUSES

Commonly referred to as "cockerel boxes", these small houses are invaluable as aids to show condition. If made 3 ft. square they will take anything from the smallest bantam to the largest big 'un and be large enough for pairs of pullets which have grown up together and not been separated.

If the houses can be contrived facing south for one lot and north for the other, those birds which have delicate colouring which easily fades or goes patchy will be greatly improved by living in the north-facing boxes during summer. Examples would be buffs, blues, wheatens and delicately marked breeds like Partridge Wyandotte females, Porcelain d'Uccles and so on.

Each house can be a miniature of the design shown in Figure 3. These houses are not fitted with small, wired-in runs. The show birds are only allowed out in the early morning or late evening under the supervision of their owner. They should be exercised individually and an area has been planned with this in mind.

It is essential that the selected, prospective show birds are exercised individually and under the constant supervision of their owner. If two or more of the inmates of the cockerel boxes are turned out in the exercising area together it is highly probable – in fact, it is "odds on" – that they will bicker and spar with each other to such an extent that one or other of them will receive head wounds. These would need time to heal and condition would be lost.

It follows that if all the cockerel boxes are occupied all the birds housed in them are not exercised every day. As long as they have adequate fresh air and plenty of good, succulent greenfood in addition to their normal diet this will do them no harm. The more sedate breeds, both large and bantam, will be helped rather than hindered by being kept more "housebound" than their more active fellows.

## FOOD STORE

A working shed, where bits and pieces of repairs to appliances, etc. can be carried out; food stored in vermin-proof bins; show schedules and catalogues dealt with and records kept, is a necessary adjunct. How big and how made are matters which only the owner can decide. It is here that concrete buildings may come into their own, being proof against gnawing rats and mice and not liable to rot.

If food bins are not made to measure they will consist of clean, galvanised dustbins with tightly fitting lids. Food should not be left in sacks which are vulnerable to stray animals.

## EXHIBITION HAMPERS

It is suggested that basket-work hampers, made by a specialist, are used. If home-made receptacles are preferred, great care should be taken to see that they are adequately ventilated. A few holes bored through plywood will not do. A series of rectangles should be cut in each wall, towards the top, and covered with wire gauze or perforated zinc. These will give better ventilation to the boxes while precluding the possibility of inquisitive children poking things through ventilating holes when boxes are stored under benches at shows. Figure 6 shows typical show hampers.

## BROODY BREAKERS

This is a most valuable piece of equipment for use chiefly in summer when exhibition hens may go broody after laying a number of eggs. It consists of a coop, about 2 ft. 6 in. cube, with a weatherproof roof and ends. The back, front and floor all consist of wire mesh. The floor is supported so that it is rigid and the front has a hinged door through which the broody is first introduced to the "breaker" and through which food and water are given. The coop is set up on legs, about 2 ft. from the ground, and is placed outdoors.

As soon as the showbird-to-be gives her first "cluck" she should be put in the broody breaker. She is given a normal diet and water but any food not eaten is taken away after each meal.

The fact that she cannot settle down comfortably and has a free circulation of air round her combine to cause the hen's maternal instincts to abate and fade away very quickly.

It is an advantage if the broody breaker is placed within sight of other birds which have normal use of their runs.

Unless the hen is exceptional she should have lost desire to sit and can be re-conditioned after about a week.

Figure 7.    Standard show baskets designed for two or
three bantams.

## HOSPITAL PEN

If this optional item is provided, it should also have a wire floor with droppings tray under it and be made on similar lines to the broody breaker, except that the back is solid. Only mild cases which will yield to treatment should be dealt with. Anything likely to be stubborn or lead to further trouble should become a subject for speedy disposal by incineration.

## CHAPTER 5

## FEEDING METHODS UNDER MODERN CONDITIONS

### ALTERNATIVE APPROACHES

THE MODERN CONDITIONS under which we live include world shortages of grain and other items which go to make up poultry feed and ever-increasing prices.

It is obvious to any thinking man that world supplies of grain and meat are being re-distributed. It follows that some material formerly processed into poultry feedstuff must become scarcer and dearer.

This means that the fancier, whose interest is not in the optimum number of eggs laid by pullets, but in the health and condition of the birds themselves, can look to alternatives to the sack of processed feed with considerable gain both in condition of stock and cash expenditure. The established menu of grain for one feed and something "straight from the bag" for another, used by many poultrymen, is capable of revision without stock suffering.

For those fanciers who are *not* prepared to go to a little trouble in the preparation of food for their exhibition poultry there is no choice. They must go on paying prices which have increased tremendously in recent times.

True, these mashes are "boosted" to prevent stress and disease found in commercial units. They are graded to meet varying appetites and economic conditions.

But such mashes are not strictly necessary for birds intended for show and some of which — far from being pushed along to lay more eggs — are held back so that they do not lay too much during the show season. Bodily condition and glossy plumage count for more than a few extra eggs in most cases.

Those prepared to give that extra care and attention which show fowls deserve may use much food that would otherwise go out as household waste. This, together with produce from the garden and peelings from vegetables prepared in the kitchen, will provide a great deal of sustenance. Balanced with cereal meal from the miller, a wet mash can be made to give bodily condition.

Fortunately, the majority of exhibition poultry are kept in such numbers that this sort of feeding is possible. Old-fashioned, maybe, and involving a little extra effort, but the end-product is very satisfying to the birds and economical to the pocket of the fancier.

I have carefully checked with established millers and food compounders that the following foodstuffs are available at the time of writing. Each merchant emphasised that stocks are liable to great fluctuations, both in availability and price.

## CATEGORIES OF FEEDING STUFFS

Food commonly used for poultry falls into three categories:

1. *Carbohydrates.* These are mainly derived from grain crops. Principal grains and their products are:

| Grain | Products |
|---|---|
| (a) Wheat | Fine wheatfeed, Pollard, Bran, Biscuit Meal. |
| (b) Oats | Ground oats, bruised oats, groats, oatmeal. |
| (c) Barley | Barley meal. |
| (d) Maize | Flaked maize, Maize meal. |

The main purposes of these foods are to provide bulk and to add body weight. They assist in growth, particularly of the bone structure, and development of plumage of young stock. The grains, used as a corn feed, maintain digestive organs in good order being relatively hard and needing more effort by the muscles to effect digestion.

2. *Proteins,* mainly derived from animal sources:

(a) Fish meal.
(b) Meat meal.
(c) Tinned cat and dog foods of reputable brands containing a high proportion of meat and fish.
(d) Household scraps of meat (raw and cooked); cheese parings and rinds; bacon rinds; bones cooked under pressure.

Protein foods provide a source of replacement following normal metabolism which constantly takes place in the body, enabling layers (particularly) to continue to develop and ripen their immature yolks so that a reasonable supply of eggs is maintained. They also assist considerably with the making of flesh and muscle and the development of plumage.

3. *Fats and Oils,* as used by the small poultry-keeper are:

(a) Cod Liver Oil.
(b) Natural oils as found in cereals, e.g., maize.
(c) Oil and fats derived from household trimmings from meat.

Not wanted in excessive amounts these items serve their useful purpose to help balance mashes and assist in conditioners.

In the methods suggested below, mash is sometimes bulked out with cooked vegetables. The best of these are potatoes, swede, turnips and carrots. All these root vegetables can be stored dry over winter and are best boiled and mashed before use.

4. *Supplementary Feedstuffs.*

Other foods which might be used in small quantities from time to time when birds are being specially conditioned, are:

(a) Hemp seed.
(b) Plain canary seed.
(c) Dari.
(d) Buckwheat.
(e) Linseed.
(f) Pea meal.

The first five items provide minor sources of oil and are chiefly valuable for keeping appetites sharp or putting a gloss on plumage. Pea meal is a vegetable protein and often favoured by exhibitors of hard feather fowls as less likely to cause their birds to become soft when wet mash is used. Some of the wheatfeed is replaced by pea meal.

## BALANCED DIET ESSENTIAL

In order to use these foods to best advantage some sort of balance must be established. The poultryman should consider the proportion of meat to other items he normally gets as the main course of a three-course meal. He will then get the picture in his mind.

Usually, he gets a portion of meat (protein), baked potato (fats and carbohydrates), mashed or boiled potatoes (carbohydrates), green vegetables (roughage, vitamins, mineral salts). The proportion of meat is probably not more than 1 : 10. This balanced meal provides all that is needful for health. What goes before is an appetiser and what follows, a sweetener, eaten for the pleasure of the diner.

Now, think of a meat sandwich. This concentrated meal has meat (protein) and bread (carbohydrates) in the proportion of about 1 : 5. Such concentrations can only be well utilised on occasion.

With these thoughts in mind the making up of economy feeds which will do all that is required of them, is not impossible. Try to keep a balanced diet so that the fowls are in good health and bodily condition; add something in the way of a sweetener as required; change over to concentrated feeding only occasionally.

The management of poultry for exhibition does not take in hatching and rearing. It should be sufficient to advise readers that the easiest and safest way to successful chick rearing is by using prepared foods.

## Examples of home-made wet mashes

1. Stale bread has been rusked in the oven and broken into pieces or biscuit meal is used. Put one or more handfuls in the bottom of a bucket and cover with cold water. Leave for a couple of hours. Drain off surplus moisture.

Add household scraps of chopped meat, bacon rinds, cheese parings, etc. to an amount that will not exceed one-tenth of the total bulk. Add fine wheatfeed and stir thoroughly until a friable mash is obtained. This must "ball together" when a handful is squeezed but fall apart when dropped. If the mash is too dry add water and mix again. This will keep adults in good health and condition, with a reasonable laying rate.

2. Put a suitable quantity of dry bran in the bucket. Add as much boiled, chopped vegetables as will be necessary to moisten total bulk of mash. Leave for an hour. Stir in fish or meat meal (but not both) equivalent to not more than 10 per cent of total bulk. Dry off with cereal meal until a friable mash is achieved. If too dry, add more boiled vegetables and stir again.

3. Use rusk or biscuit meal as the base, as in example 1. Add cod liver oil at rate of 1 teaspoonful for 6 birds. Add

cereal meals and dry off until good consistency is achieved. Then stir in chopped meat scrap, etc., from the household until the mash becomes friable.

Birds will very rarely tire of fine wheatfeed in their wet mash.

They would become stale if constantly fed with any of the other cereals *ad lib.* It is better to mix them in the ratio 2 parts wheatfeed; 1 part oats; ½ part barley or maize meal. The balance is better; taste is better; consistency of the mash is better.

These examples demonstrate that reasonable balance can be achieved in different ways. On those days when there is no household scrap protein available, fish or meat meals are used. When there are boiled vegetables, water is not added. When vegetables are used, which are probably a bit sloppy in consistency, bran is used as a base as this "opens up" the mixture far better than biscuit meal. Keeping a 1 : 7 ratio in mind, the poultryman will usually be able to achieve some economy and vary mash to the needs of his stock, sharpening appetites and keeping birds really fit by always serving a palatable feed.

I have the idea that poultry are more sensitive to the taste and manner of preparation of their food than some poultrymen may think. Keynote, therefore, is palatability. Different mixes should be tried until that which is most readily taken is found. This becomes the staple diet and variations are made in order to "ring the changes".

Breed has something to do with future management. If a large, heavy breed is favoured it must be well-grown and well-conditioned when put on show. Intake of food and crop capacity are critical factors. A small eater will not grow really massive.

Light breeds, with fully flowing plumage, should be brought to maturity less slowly. They will, in fact, benefit from a slightly greater amount of protein and oils to help plumage grow smoothly and quickly. Even so, they must not be lightly fleshed at maturity but have enough on their bones to be able to withstand travelling to shows and penning for two or three days at a time.

In both cases it is advisable to have a rearing programme which includes wet mash daily. Growers, segregated as to sex, should be kept in appropriate groups. There is positive disadvantage in putting birds of different natures in the same pen. Slow growing heavy breeds might be put together without harm; light breeds with head adornments, e.g., Anconas, Leghorns, could run together. Hard feathered breeds would not be run in the same pen with soft feathered birds. Commonsense at this point will save damage to prospective show birds and enable feeding methods to be adjusted.

## Growing stock from eight weeks old

At about eight weeks of age, young stock will need four feeds daily. A reasonable feed of corn in the morning, the birds being encouraged to exercise by scattering the corn in the floor litter so that the birds have to scratch to get it, will give them a fair start to the day.

If the birds are not on a grass run they will need fresh greenfood daily. This can consist of the surplus leaves from any green garden vegetables. Washed and chopped, the greenstuff is given from a trough about mid-day and a very small feed of growers' pellets (ready-made food from manufacturers) added.

Alternative sources of greenfood are freshly cut, spring grass; chickweed; mustard and cress, grown in boxes; sprouted oats, grown in boxes; roots of swedes, split down the middle so that the flesh can be pecked out. In high summer there should also be lettuce, grown specially for the birds.

The teatime feed can consist of wet mash, given in a trough and left before the birds for twenty minutes. If they have ravenously eaten all the mash before that time elapses they should be given a little more, and, again, a second helping until either the birds have ceased eating or the time is up. Should the first supply prove to be too great then the surplus should be taken away and the amount adjusted the following day.

It may seem that this time is too exacting and no great harm will be done if the birds eat up quicker or food is left a little longer. Careful observation will show that growers soon establish their own natural pecking order and the same birds are always to the fore in about the same positions at the trough.

When they have had their fill and stopped bickering they

turn away and birds which are timid by nature are able to come forward and get their share.

This eating "by rota" takes about twenty minutes and the time is reasonably critical to successful feeding of birds which are all intended to gain best bodily condition at maturity.

The alternative to trough feeding is to scatter mash over a wide area so that each bird has room in which to eat without being jostled from its ration by another. I have seen this method used but its drawbacks seem to me to outweigh any advantages chiefly that many crumbs are left for sparrows and other birds which may carry disease.

At this early growing stage a ready-made growers' mash, with a base of soaked biscuit meal, will serve best, and make for a good foundation.

The final, late evening feed, given by artificial light in the early part of the season, consists of a little grain alternated with a little of the home-made wet mash. The birds need just as much as will put them comfortably "to bed".

As soon as the mid-day feed can be saved and growers have large enough crops to be comfortable until the next feed comes along, this should be done.

Good feeding does not equate with over-feeding. The latter will defeat its own ends by making birds lethargic whereas they are wanted active and fit, their food helping to maximise growth.

**From twelve weeks old**

From about twelve weeks of age only greenfood should be provided at noon. Nor is there need to continue to shred and feed this material from a trough. As long as it is tender and palatable any greenfood should be hung at head height of the birds concerned and they will enjoy pecking pieces from what is on offer. Tough stuff should not be given anyway as it is liable to cause crop or intestinal troubles.

With good management, growing stock should be thriving and the final, supplementary feed can be withdrawn when the birds are about four months old.

Staple diet is then grain in the morning; greens at noon; wet mash in the afternoon and just a suggestion of a little extra grain when the evening inspection is carried out.

The method used by John Wharton, that famous breeder of large Wyandottes, which proved so successful for him, will bear description. He made a wet mash containing a fairly high proportion of wheatings. This he divided into portions, each of which was large enough to be formed into a round "cake" about 9 inches across and 2 or 3 inches deep. He then added about one quarter of the bulk of large, white maize and kneaded each "cake" until the grain was evenly incorporated with the mash. The "cakes" were then placed on top of a stove to warm through.

At the afternoon feed each "cake" was broken into pieces and given to a pen of Mr. Wharton's exhibition White Wyandottes. He explained to me (when I interviewed him on behalf of POULTRY WORLD) that some birds always bustled forward and quickly filled their crops. These, being satisfied, then withdrew from near their feeder and others could get a feed, largely from the maize which tended to fall away from the mash on impact with the ground.

Additionally, the mixed feed lasted better than would mash during the long winter nights of North Yorkshire where his famous stud was housed.

It ought to be stated that his stock had the benefit of extensive grass runs and his ground was lightly stocked. These two points are essential if this method is to be successfully used.

## LINSEED CONDITIONING

As a general aid to good plumage, the use of boiled linseed is strongly recommended once weekly from about four months old until plumage is fully grown. Less base than usual is soaked and got ready for the mash. The difference between the amount of base used and the normal quantity is made up with additional wheatfeed, needed to dry off the mash when linseed is used, as it is rather sticky.

### Method

Place some linseed in a pan and cover with cold water. Place on heat and bring to the boil, then simmer slowly for two hours or so. The result will be a jelly-like mass which should be allowed to cool. No attempt should be made to store the jelly from one week to another or it will become sour. The pan or other vessel in which it has been cooked should be thoroughly cleansed after use. Add the usual meals to the base, then a quantity of linseed jelly and stir well together until the right consistency is achieved. No liquid will be necessary. The linseed should not be given more than once weekly or it will prove laxative. When used in reasonable quantity and regularly it has a beneficial effect on the growth of feathers.

## FEEDING AND MATURITY

At the point of maturity, stock will be on two full meals daily, plus greenfood. Poultrymen must use their discretion, based on observation of the way stock is developing, as to whether a little extra food should be given at night.

In the main, I would prefer not to see this done as a keen, rather hungry bird will respond better when brought in for final, individual conditioning ready for showday. It is then that other items shown in the food list will be employed and their use is described in Chapter 8.

## EXCEPTIONS TO REARING METHODS

Hard feather birds, like Old English Game and Indian Game, need special consideration. The nature of their plumage and the muscular formation of their bodies demand that they have a lesser quantity of wet mash which is normally relied on to provide the ingredients for good development of plumage. Management for them will include maximum freedom of range and exercise to keep muscles taut and trim and ensure development across the shoulders. Their staple diet will consist of grain, chiefly hard wheat. They can also have clipped oats and kibbled maize, with a small proportion of barley. Their wet mash, given not more than twice weekly, will have additional protein or this may be given in the form of chopped, cooked meat offal.

With bantams the hard feathered breeds are treated as above. All the rest, without exception, are better if maturing early. A slow-growing bantam is bound to make a larger specimen and when it comes to the crunch of critical selection, then the bigger the bantam the smaller the prize.

The early layer is usually fine-boned, bodily development stopping soon after the first egg is laid. Let them mature quickly for minimum size, feeding generously as to quality but moderately as to quantity.

## SUPPLEMENTARY PROTEINS

As fish and meat meal are at exceptionally high cost nowadays, it will pay to establish contact with a local butcher who may be able to supply offal such as beast heart, lights, pluck and so on, usually sold to dog breeders. Only enough should be got as can be used quickly unless the poultryman is prepared to store some of the cooked meat in his deep-freezer.

The best way, after cleaning the worst of the "rough stuff" from such butchers' offal is to steam it for as long as is needed to make it tender, then mince and add to the mash.

The same could be done with fish heads and trimmings from the process of filleting, as an alternative to fish meal. Some shops now sell processed dog meat by the pound and this could also be used.

In no case should these foods be given more liberally than outlined as the amount of protein necessary for a wet mash.

Figure 8.   Large Buff Laced Wyandotte Pullet (Winner: National Championship Show — S. J. Rickard)

# CHAPTER 6

## COMPOSITION AND MANAGEMENT OF BREEDING PENS

### GOOD PARENT STOCK ESSENTIAL

THE WINNING OF prizes actually starts in the breeding pens. Although we have skipped the mechanics of hatching eggs and rearing chicks to the growing stage, we cannot ignore the fine art of selecting the parent stock from which future prizewinners are to spring.

### GENERAL RULE

The general rule is that show poultry are bred from prizeworthy parents. The exception is in those double-mated breeds where the "breeding" sex must, of necessity, be bred from show quality stock of that sex which is normally exhibited.

No matter what breed is favoured, when breeding pens are being put together the sort which takes prizes at shows must be favoured, if success is to follow.

The chief reason is not far to seek. Take headpoints as an example. There are many different shapes and sizes of single combs and nearly as many more of rosecombs. It does not do merely to have a single combed sire if the Standard and the judges who interpret it can only be satisfied with a comb of a certain size, shape and texture.

The only way of knowing that combs are desirable is to show against others. If points are consistently lost on account of formation of combs, then active steps must be taken to remedy matters, either by an outcross to some winning specimen which can be bought or by patient and careful selection from the home stud.

Look at the other end of a show fowl — the tail. Does it have the circling sickle feathers of the large Game cock or the compact adornments of the Orpington? Is plumage firm and boldly carried or very soft and pliable? The Standard for the breed will say what the ideal is. Current wins at shows will demonstrate what judges favour most. Winning specimens must come somewhere near what's wanted and it is little use including something else in the breeding pen.

It is true that parent stock can be selected at home by careful comparison with the Breed Standards. It is in the interpretation of the Standards that differences of opinion can occur. It is little use being dogmatic over some detail of the Standard and making this a prime consideration when selecting the breeding pen if the same point is taken for granted by the majority of judges and some other detail highly regarded as necessary to the winning of prizes.

It is essential, therefore, to exhibit fairly regularly so as to be conversant with current trends in one's chosen breed and select parent stock according to their likelihood in producing winners.

Some strains of exhibition poultry show a marked tendency to breed better males than females and vice versa, even in a self coloured variety. Where this trait is firmly fixed it is necessary for the breeder to note carefully the chief winners in the opposite sex to that well produced at home and compare their exhibits in the same sex as the home-bred winners.

It may be very beneficial to get a good specimen of that opposite sex to blend in the home breeding pen and so break the sequence of winners in one sex only.

For instance, suppose the home stud habitually produces better pullets than cockerels in Buff Orpingtons. When exhibited, home-bred pullets are always near the head of their class but cockerels do not get higher than, say, third or fourth. If another exhibitor shows males which often win their class while his pullets sometimes run second, then his level of performance is better and a good male from that exhibitor would most probably improve the results from a breeding pen by providing winners in both sexes.

## Exceptions to Rule

A limited number of breeds are so constituted that it is impossible to produce winning males and females from the parents.

This is because Standards have been so drawn up that one or the other of the two sexes (although the natural mates of the opposite sex in the same breed) are not acceptable for exhibition. Thus, a Brown Leghorn cockerel with upright comb, all-black tail and bright top colour with sound black striping can only be bred from females which have the same points in diminished degree — but these are *not* female show points. Winning pullets, on the other hand, are bred from males which resemble them by having falling combs and dull colouring which would not allow them to win prizes.

Stock producing show cockerels are known as cock (or cockerel) breeders and the parents of exhibition pullets are referred to as "pullet" (but never "hen") breeders.

It is possible to double-mate — as this process is termed — any existing breed either for colour or headpoints or other features and it was, once, the fashion to do so. Experience has proved that this troublesome and expensive method of producing show poultry is quite unnecessary except for a few varieties which have differing Standard requirements as described immediately above.

The full list of varieties which must be double-mated for real success at exhibition is:—

Dark Brahma
Partridge Cochin
Gold Pencilled Hamburgh
Silver Pencilled Hamburgh
Gold Spangled Hamburgh*
Silver Spangled Hamburgh*
Black Leghorn
Brown Leghorn
Black Minorca (for headpoints)
Modern Game*
Black Wyandotte
Partridge Wyandotte
Silver Pencilled Wyandotte
Laced Wyandotte*

*Formerly strictly double-mated for perfection of markings but present trends are for single-mated pens to be used and allowances made in the fine detail of feather pattern, when these varieties are met at shows.

## NEW BREEDERS

When new breeders select their early pens they are attracted first to this merit then to that. They tend to include birds of startling virtue in some point even if deficient in others. In short, they are "carried away" by something

41

they think eminently desirable.

The result is that their breeding pens are uneven because owners have tried to cover the whole gamut of desirable points in some six or seven fowls. Progeny will also be uneven, varying from the good one which has thrown together all the parental virtues to many which are not wanted because they show more faults than merits.

### Family likeness

Now, take a look at the No. 1 pen of any experienced breeder whose stock has been consistently at the top for some years. Heads will all look alike, even down to the minor point of expression in face. They may not be 100 per cent perfect and there may be a blemish common to all but general likeness will be there in the breeding stock. Bodies will be of similar shape and size; tails will be recognisable as all bred from one stud; feet and legs will be strictly comparable. Plumage will be almost as good in one bird as another and colour and/or markings about the same in every bird.

The "old hand" knows what he has got. He knows what his stock will produce and tries to improve a little each year by selection. Even in those leaner years when his birds do not quite reach expectations he does not rush about seeking new blood. Instead he selects the best of what he has and puts them aside for next season's breeding pen.

All this is because his stock has been inbred to produce a "family likeness" which is easily recognisable both by him and many of the judges whose job it is to award prizes at the leading shows.

Figure 7 shows a family group of Orpington Bantams which breed true to type with very little variation.

## INBREEDING

If properly applied, inbreeding is not a weakening process which ruins the constitutions of exhibition poultry nor is it a form of magic which can produce good birds from moderate parents.

All the points which are needed for prizewinning must appear, in some degree, in the original stock upon which the stud is founded. By mating together related birds and not introducing new breeding stock in a haphazard or casual

Figure 9.. Family likeness exhibited by a pen of Black Orpington bantams. (Bred by Mr. Will Burdett).

manner, selection enables the breeder to emphasise the best points and repress the worst of those points which were originally "locked in".

Inbreeding does not give new and better points of perfection. It keeps available those which exist and helps to maintain them in a dominant state.

Because of the relatively small number of birds usual in a fancier's pens it is possible for him to run the risk of getting all his birds related in exactly the same degree, at a very early stage.

## Mated pairs

If he is prepared to do some careful book-keeping and exact pedigree breeding he can overcome this drawback by mating of individual pairs. Many birds (particularly large, heavy breeds) would be infertile if a pair were put together and left all day long. Supervision of the time a pair runs together will enable the breeder to know when the birds have mated and they can re-occupy their own houses, the female's eggs being marked and her chicks toe-punched or wing-banded when hatched.

Should time not be available for such supervision there is a simple remedy at hand; make up a quartette with two other hens laying eggs of a different colour. Keep and hatch only the wanted eggs and use the others for eating.

Should it be part of the plan to have chicks from one good hen but more than one male it should be borne in mind that she will continue to produce chicks sired by the first male for about a fortnight after last being served by him.

## Successful relationships

By the means outlined it is possible to keep exact pedigrees and to judge the degree of relationship to a nicety. Aim, as far as possible, for an uncle/niece or nephew/aunt mating as likeliest to fix whatever points have been particularly selected each season.

Repetition of the points by some exceptional winner can probably be achieved by working towards a grandfather/granddaughter pairing (when the male was the champion) or a grandson/grandmother mating (when the hen was the big winner).

## Two pen system

If other methods do not suit because of absolute lack of time at home to watch over the behaviour of the breeding pens, continuance of the "family likeness" can be carried on for some years by mating two pens each season, as evenly balanced in character and numbers as possible.

The male heading Pen A is chosen from the cockerels bred by Pen B and vice versa, the pullets remaining in their home ground, so to speak.

By strict selection for conformation and health and the instant rejection of stock which is downright poor in appearance (regardless of back-breeding) quite good results can be had this way.

## FEEDING

As far as condition goes, it should be appreciated that breeding stock does not want as much or as rich food as when in process of growing plumage or being conditioned for show.

Breeding stock should be lean rather than fat; hard and active instead of lazy and contented. At the same time females must have sufficient protein, greenfood, grit and clean water in their diet to enable them to lay soundly shelled and well formed eggs.

Since much breeding of fancy fowls takes place in the natural laying period of Springtime, any tendency to give *extra* protein to induce egg laying at the maximum rate should be resisted.

Ensure exercise by scattering the morning grain in the floor litter and making the birds work really hard to get it.

Since breeding hens are likely to sustain broken plumage, by visits to the nest boxes and the attentions of the male as well as being weathered by running freely outdoors, there is no point in trying to keep them in good feather by giving additional feeds at night or shading them during the day.

Let them run so that plumage may become as shabby as it likes. If any of the hens go broody and are allowed to sit they will moult while with their chicks and come through like the proverbial "new pin". Others can be force moulted at a later date, as can the sire who is likely to be rather battle-worn before his stint of breeding is over.

An additional bonus which follows the use of show birds in the breeding pens is that, being lean, they will condition up wonderfully well once they have moulted and will last throughout an autumn season of indoor shows.

Figure 10.  Old English Pheasant Fowl

# CHAPTER 7

## REARING IN SMALL UNITS

### PLANNING ACCOMMODATION

WITH THE SEXES separated at, say, eight weeks old, growing stock should be put in suitable groups, according to the accommodation available. It pays big dividends to have rested grass runs in which the growers can run until they start to assume their final plumage.

Birds of widely differing ages should not be mixed. It is natural for the stronger fowls to eat freely while denying the smaller, weaker chicks their full share of food. This can only mean that while the big get bigger, small growers cease to thrive and will be below normal size at maturity.

How many should be run in each group depends on how many were hatched at one time and how large are the houses and runs available. There can be no hard and fast rule for all breeds in all circumstances.

### SEGREGATION

Within a fairly short time the birds which are best in general properties will show up and they should be segregated at about fourteen weeks of age.

At this point they cannot be housed individually nor would they thrive well if they were. Batches of growers should be chosen on quality. The exercise of some stockmanship now becomes essential. If the group contains a bully it should associate only with the larger and stronger growers which can take care of themselves. The slower eater, always low in the pecking order, should not be put in with her.

Keep an eye open for the later maturing specimen which, in the end, comes along to beat all the others on sheer quality. She will have been left with the main batch but should be taken up for better conditioning, along with one or two of her mates, as soon as her quality is apparent.

Maturity and showtime both approach together and something can be done to get them to coincide if the most forward of the birds in groups are put in "cockerel boxes" in pairs. Two together make company for each other and there will be some competition for food thus promoting good health and high condition.

Until one or both are taken up for individual conditioning and pen training, the pairs can live together quite happily. After they have been apart a watchful eye will have to be given to see that they do not bicker and damage each other when put together again.

## COCKERELS

Cockerels in most breeds can run longer and will mature later than their sisters. For a short time after weaning a batch of cockerels will manage quite well together and should be run in a group.

As soon as the first couple of birds assert themselves, usually when crowing becomes established among the most forward cockerels, trouble in the form of damaged combs and lobes will quickly follow their initial sparring for mastery.

It is at this time that an adult cock can be put in charge. The "policeman" will tolerate only that juvenile sparring which is fairly harmless. As soon as real bickering starts — which appears to be a challenge to his authority — he quells it with a few well directed kicks and flaps.

Only when the lusty cockerels are well grown and the adult cock is going into moult should it be necessary to take him away and pen the potential winners singly.

More than the usual care should be paid to those breeds which have white earlobes. Should any of them sustain a sharp peck on the smooth surface of the lobe it will discolour and may even become puckered as a result. These breeds have, necessarily, to be housed singly at a rather earlier age than the large, heavies.

## SHADING FROM THE SUN

When adult feathers peep through, about sixteen weeks onwards, light shade should be provided during the height of the sun's power from Springtime onwards. If birds run out in all weather their new plumage will become bleached in bright sunlight and their final garb be patchy, the first-grown feathers being weathered and the later ones not.

Old-timers, giving their birds attention during many hours of the day, used to allow them to run in the early morning and again in the evening, when the sun was low in the sky. It is unfortunate that few people have time to "stand and stare" nowadays. So much can be learned merely by observing stock that time spent just watching the birds is fully justified. Apart from seeing that selected show stock does nothing silly, like indulging in a dust bath when soil is slightly damp and the bird is merely intended to have a few minutes air and exercise, things like deportment, action, wing and ·tail carriage, can all be noted and the information stored away for future use.

If time is available I thoroughly recommend that owners are present whenever their show birds are given an outing, in the early morning and evening for preference.

Today's exhibitors, probably away from home for most of the day, must contrive houses with maximum ventilation and light screens of canvas or similar porous material to cover the wire netted ventilators so as to create shade and prevent sun's rays falling directly on to plumage. This is particularly desirable for soft colours like buffs and blues. Plastic sheeting will not act in the same way since it does not admit air.

An important point is that the screens should be placed over the outside of any windows so as to prevent the sun striking the glass and causing an undue rise in temperature.

## FEEDING

Feeding methods do not need to be altered until the birds are individually housed and being got ready for some specific date. They should not be overfed because their exercise will be limited. Show birds need regular supplies of fresh greenfood.

A smaller, evening feed given in the presence of the fancier will do much to gentle the birds and make them amenable to handling for exhibition.

While plumage is growing, however, they should not be picked up and handled to a great degree. It is only after feathers are fully grown that fowls can tolerate this readily. While most of their plumage is still in quill they are best left alone.

# CHAPTER 8

## CONDITIONING FOR THE SHOWPEN

### STAGES IN CONDITIONING

PREVIOUS CHAPTERS have stressed that the exhibitor should know his birds as individuals. It is more important than before that he should deal with his birds individually, at this stage.

To prepare a fowl for exhibition, so that it has utmost fitness and is clean and attractive, it is necessary to proceed in proper order. The process should not be dragged out, or the bird will become stale, nor can it be hurried. The main stages involved are as follows:

1. Pen Training.

2. Special Feeding.

3. Preparation of Plummage.

4. Grooming Unwashed Birds.

5. Preparing White Earlobes.

6. Management in the Moult.

### PEN TRAINING

Training is given so that the selected bird is steady in the showpen, shows itself to best advantage and is readily assessed by the judge.

A showpen of appropriate size being available in the penning house, its floor should be covered with clean, white sawdust and there should be a drinking vessel, fixed so that the drinking water in it cannot be spilt.

At dusk, the chosen showbird is brought from its cockerel box (where it has already been quietly treated for some little time) and placed in the confines of the showpen. It should be gently placed, head-first within the pen, and the door closed.

Unless the bird has already been fully fed, a small amount of grain may be given and the fowl left severely alone until the following morning. It is then fed in the normal way and left throughout the day.

On the evening of the second day, the poultryman gives the bird a part feed of some favourite food. He then gently pops a light cane or judging stick through the bars of the

Figure 11.  Trained to show off style - a Black-red
Modern Game cockerel.
(Photograph by the late A.E. Brust [U.S.A.]).

pen and causes the bird to move around and assume a pose appropriate to the breed.

All the while he speaks, quietly and meaningfully. After a few minutes of this treatment and a little more of the appetising food, the bird is left, care being taken to see that there is a sufficiency of drinking water available.

Later, by artificial light if necessary, some titbit like chopped meat, bread and milk or something of that nature may be given. Confidence and the association of food as a reward for co-operation have been established.

Day 3 and the chosen exhibit will have settled wonderfully well, coming to the front of the pen for food when the owner makes his presence known.

At this stage, before being fed in the evening, the bird should be "set up" by hand and posed in the style usual to winners in the breed.

In Figure 8 it will be seen that the Black-red Modern Game Cockerel is stretching himself to his full height thus emphasising the features required of a winner. Note the long legs, whip tail and small body.

**Examples**

1. A *Modern Game* would be gently stroked across the shoulders, down the back and over the tail, then touched under the beak and wattles to cause it to stretch upwards and show its "reach".

2. A *Wyandotte* would have its stern raised and its head lifted just sufficiently to show off frontal as well as rear curves.

3. *Indian Game* are encouraged to stand "wide" with legs well apart.

4. *Pekin* bantams must be thoroughly docile so that their cushions can be moulded into ball shape by hand pressure while the birds are induced to carry* their heads fairly low, their bodies tilting slightly forward.

To each breed give enough attention and stroking to get it to assume best style. Gentle talk flows, all the while.

It should be appreciated that, in some breeds, the Standard demands different carriage when males and females are compared. For instance, Faverolles males' tails have to be "somewhat upright" while their mates should be carried "midway between upright and drooping". In the Standard for Houdans the scale of points differs, feature by feature, and emphasis is shifted when each sex is considered.

Other examples will be known to those who have closely studied the Standard for their own particular breed and such knowledge put to practical use when training specimens in the penning room.

## Special Feeding

Normal food is given in slightly reduced quantity at this point. Later in the evening, a supplementary feed is given, varying with the needs of the bird. If a young one which still wants more flow of plumage, then a generous quantity of bread and milk to which has been added two or three drops of cod liver oil will help. All not eaten should be removed; none being left in the pen.

A pale faced bird, not yet in full condition, would benefit from a feed of stale sponge cake moistened with port or claret wine. A lean bird should be given a heavy mash containing plenty of wheatfeed while a fat one, apart from being dieted, should have more protein in the form of meat or fish scrap, boiled and minced.

Most bantams and all Game fowl get extra gloss if they can be induced to eat small quantities of plain canary seed or hempseed. Black, red and other strongly coloured birds which do not need washing for show gain their radiant gloss from little feeds of prepared, tinned cat food, such as can be found in any pet shop or supermarket. This sort of food can now be got in different flavours. By varying them, appetites can be kept sharp. The protein and vitamin content is usually similar in all the tins.

## Bread and Milk Conditioning

Exhibitors have complained to me that they cannot get birds to take bread and milk; it is always sticky and dirty. Had they followed this method, they would not have had such an experience.

Stale bread should be rusked in a slow oven. The rusk is broken into pieces about pea size for bantams and hazel nut size for large fowls. Broken rusk is covered with cold water (this is most important: do *not* scald it) until thoroughly moistened. Surplus water is then squeezed out. A few drops of cod liver oil are dropped on the wet rusk and a spoonful of sugar added. The whole is then covered with as much milk (or dried milk powder made into solution) as it will absorb — and no more.

Bread and milk is best fed from a shallow wooden tray which is taken away and washed after each meal. There is nothing, but nothing, to equal this for wealth of feather and maintenance of bodily condition.

## PREPARATION OF PLUMAGE

Except with birds which are newly matured and absolutely at "twelve o' clock" in health and condition, there is usually a feather or two slightly damaged through normal, natural causes. If these are left in and the judge finds them he is, quite rightly, entitled to deduct the odd point under the heading of "condition". While not advocating wholesale plucking (which would be detected anyway) I know that the removal of such damaged small, body feathers is usually allowed.

Large wing and tail feathers should not be removed. Their absence would create so glaring a defect that judges would have natural suspicions as to the soundness of such feathers before removal and act accordingly.

In many breeds with intricate markings there are always some foul feathers among the many good ones. It is usual for these to be taken out so as to present a more level and evenly marked bird for the judge's appraisal, he knowing what allowance to make in this matter.

On the strict letter of the law anything calculated to deceive a judge is not permissible. But custom has blessed the practice and it is no use the novice showing his birds exactly "as hatched" in a variety where it is usual to dress the plumage before exhibiting.

Instances where such dressing greatly improves an exhibit include Partridge marked varieties and their allied Silver Pencilleds (including Dark Brahmas). In males it is chiefly the hackles which have feathers bearing faulty stripes which are removed and, perhaps, a few breast feathers which carry a tinge of colour on them. Female plumage must be carefully scrutinised and any feathers with "broken" pencilling removed. These are especially to be found in the cushion, towards the tail coverts.

Pencilled Hamburgh females can always be improved to gain regularity of markings (by removing feathers which are coarse and broken in their pencilling) if those feathers with V-shaped markings are taken out to leave the others with straight barrings in the majority.

It would be a miracle if a Barred Rock of either sex were shown exactly as bred. It is a "racing certainty" that any bird of good ground colour and bold markings also has a number of dark or black feathers in its plumage. These are, invariably, removed before the bird is exhibited. Cuckoo varieties, while not as precise in their pattern, ought to be looked over for dark or light feathers also.

Speckled (tri-coloured) and Mottled (including Anconas) can, manifestly, have the regularity of their markings improved by the removal of crowded feathers or those bearing blobs and other irregularly shaped markings. Some Laced varieties similarly gain by the removal of feathers which overlap others too much and Spangled Hamburghs certainly do.

The softer coloured self varieties, like buffs and blues, sometimes grow a few feathers which are paler in shade than the rest of their plumage thus giving a mottled appearance, and these are removed bodily.

When checking marked varieties for foul feathers it is wise, when one is found, to look in exactly the same place on the opposite side of its body. For instance, a black feather in a cuckoo variety might be first found on the left side of the cushion, about mid-way towards the tail. Immediately, the same point should be scrutinised on the right side of the cushion and it is more likely than not that a similarly defective feather will be found.

It should be made clear that what I have written refers to small body feathers only: just a few of them on otherwise tip-top specimens. No amount of plucking will make a badly marked bird into a good one. Large wing and tail feathers, no matter how dismarked, must not be removed. In no circumstances must scissors be used to cut off plumage.

Dressing — although strictly illegal — must be left to the individual consciences of exhibitors although, as I say, it is generally regarded as permissible when done in moderation with an eye to improving the overall appearance of an exhibit.

## GROOMING UNWASHED BIRDS

Dark coloured birds, which do not need a bath, should receive some attention to heighten the brilliance of their plumage. If they have become slightly muddy the adhering dirt should be allowed to dry out thoroughly. It can then be removed by very gently brushing — down the feather and not across it — with a fine wire brush as sold for use on suede shoes.

Afterwards a piece of silk, old and worn for preference, should be used as a pad and passed gently and quickly down the plumage several times for two or three nights in succession. Any birds free from soiling can also have this treatment with the silk pad to improve gloss.

Heads and legs of all intended showbirds should be washed and groomed as detailed in the next chapter, and this applies to dark coloured birds groomed as set out above just as much as to those which are newly washed.

## CARE OF WHITE EARLOBES

Breeds such as Minorcas, Leghorns, Rosecomb bantams and others whose Standard demands that their earlobes should be white, smooth and open need extra care when being conditioned for show.

In the "good old — bad old — days" it was common for them (especially Minorcas and big, beefy White Leghorns) to be shown with a film of white ointment and/or powder on the surface of their lobes. This practice has largely died out and winners in white-lobed breeds are likely to have a natural surface to their lobes.

Such white earlobes are subject to blistering and reddening if they are exposed to the weather or lobes are allowed to become dirty or wet, so attracting a film of dust and grit. Obviously, birds must be protected from the weather as

Figure 12.  Immaculate white earlobes in a champion
Black Minorca bantam pullet.
(Property of Mr. R.G. Spencer)

soon as lobes develop. They should be prevented from bickering and sustaining pecked lobes. Weathering would show as
"blushing" of red on to the otherwise white surface; pecking
would cause a scar. In bad cases lobes could become puckered.

Blistering is associated with a dusty house or too high
living with not enough greenfood in the diet.

When these breeds are being conditioned it is essential
first to wash their lobes gently with mild soap and warm
water. They should then be patted dry with a soft, absorbent
towel. Afterwards the lobes should be thinly covered with a
good *white* talcum powder free from some of the additives
which may occur in powder made for the fashion market.
Bearing in mind the job a Baby Powder has to do, it would
be wise to use such a product.

The coating of powder means there is a soft, thin film to
prevent a coarser film of dust and grit from adhering and
causing irritation. The washing, drying and powdering should
be repeated every second day. On no account should new

powder be put over the old layer.

Before a show, all traces of powder are washed away, the lobes dried and presented to the judge in a natural state. This may be seen from the photograph of the Black Minorca Female (Figure 9).

## THE MOULT

The annual moult is a process natural to all poultry over a year old. In late summer and autumn the old, worn feathers are released from their anchorage and fall to the ground as naturally as leaves fall from the trees. They have served their purpose by protecting their wearers for a year, and are now redundant.

New feathers, tightly encased in sheaths grow through the skin in the same tracts as the old ones, and replace them. These new feathers expand as they grow and are finally free from their retaining sheaths when they have attained full length.

At this point the bird is again fully protected from the weather and can usefully live through another year of productivity, the process of the moult having taken something like two months.

A limited amount of control can be exercised over when and how the moult takes place, to the advantage of the exhibitor. But his main worry is not when a bird will moult but how it can be managed that all new plumage is smooth and of one uniform appearance.

Those birds which have been selected for controlled (or "hand") moultings should be placed in one small group in a house which they alone occupy. Their normal feed of grain is given, but nourishing wet mash is withdrawn. Greenfood and water are still given. After a few days, the total intake of food is slightly reduced. Birds are kept on such short rations until feathers drop freely, often in about ten days.

Any broken wing feathers and worn or broken tail feathers are not likely to drop as readily as the rest of the plumage. They must, therefore, be removed by hand, the process spreading over several days for each bird.

At this stage moulting fowls have a "hedgehog" like appearance and should not be handled. They lose condition in head and females stop laying. The stubby quills each contain a new feather and these will be grown smoothly and beautifully if the birds are now switched to a high protein diet. Just as food was scaled down to create conditions to encourage the moult so it should be built up again so that new plumage can be produced quickly and well.

Appetites may be a little jaded due to lack of condition and overfeeding should be guarded against or the greedier fowls will come through their moult too fat. Linseed jelly should be added to the wet mash (see Chapter 5) as an aid to smooth plumage.

Scales on legs are also removed during the moult and when birds are sufficiently feathered that they can be handled without causing discomfort, time should be taken to remove old scales from both front and back of the shanks. This is quite easily done by applying pressure with the thumb nail to the edge of each scale, causing the old covering to "spring off" to reveal the new, fully coloured scale below. Some scales drop naturally, of course. It is only the horny, semi-transparent scales which still adhere which need to be removed by hand.

# CHAPTER 9

## WASHING FOR SHOW

### SHOW PREPARATION

ALL LIGHT COLOURED poultry and some which have a dark background but with white tippings to their feathers, e.g. Millefleur d'Uccles, benefit from a thorough wash before being exhibited. Incidentally, a maturing cockerel of a heavy breed which is slow to "let down its hackle" or a moulted adult which is not gaining condition quickly enough can be helped if they are given a thorough bath, no matter what colour they are.

Modern conditions may help the poultry exhibitor with birds to wash. Deep kitchen sinks, constant hot water, well-equipped bathrooms are all available for use if convenient.

The method described below can be used in all circumstances regardless of whether water has to be heated over a domestic fire or whether modern methods are available.

**Equipment needed**
1. 3 baths or other containers of suitable size.
2. 1 large jug or other container, to ladle water.
3. 1 small sponge.
4. 2 large sponges.
5. 2 absorbent towels.
6. 1 nail brush.
7. Soap flakes and a cake of soap.
8. Sharpened orange sticks or matchsticks.

These items are needed by the fancier working solo. If he has the benefit of an assistant to rinse out and re-fill the bath, sponges, etc., he can, of course, work with less equipment.

**Method**

Take the bird and place it under the left arm, head forward. Restrain the wings by gentle pressure from the elbow. Hold the shanks forward, keeping them firmly controlled by the left hand. Give the shanks and feet a preliminary sponge down to remove the worst of the dirt, taking care that drippings do not go into the bath. Thoroughly wet the brush and draw it across the cake of soap. Then scrub the shanks and feet, front

nd back, passing the bristles across the legs and not up and
lown them. Rinse with clean water.

Bath No. 1 contains sufficient warm water to enable the
owl's body (except its head) to be immersed. The jug con-
ains very warm water in which soap flakes have been dis-
olved.

Place the bird in the bath, head towards the operator, and
hold its wings firmly down to its sides. With a large sponge,
quickly and thoroughly wet all its plumage. Now pour over
some of the dissolved soap and let it be soaking into the
plumage.

With the small sponge, lightly soaped, clean all the headpoints and immediately rinse them. The small sponge is then
rinsed in cold water and the bird made comfortable by giving
its head and face a final wipe over.

The large sponge is now carrying a good load of soapy
water and is used to clean the head feathers, then down the
neck hackle and on to the shoulders. A little more soap
solution is used and gentle rubbing, always with and not
across the grain of the feather, ensures that the bird is clean
from the top of the breast and down its front to a point between the thighs. It is possible that additional soapy water
will be wanted for the back and across the shoulders. Keep
renewing the load in the sponge and well wash down the back,
towards the tail. Then spread each wing in turn and ensure
that main flight feathers and the fluff under the wings are
properly washed. The underparts, thighs and then the tail
are also soaked and rubbed. The bird should now be lifted up
and as much of the lather removed from it as can be
accomplished by sweeping the free hand over each part of the
plumage in the order just described.

Water in Bath No. 2 is not quite as warm as in the first one
and the bird should be stood in it, as before. The second large
sponge is used to rinse out as much of the soapy water as
possible. The routine is as for Bath No. 1 but efforts are
directed to removing the soap previously applied.

Bath No. 3 contains water which is just lukewarm and
further rinsing takes place there. If the exhibit has white
plumage the addition of a very little household washing blue
can be made to heighten purity of colour when the bird is dry.
For all other varieties, nothing should be added to the third
bath.

The thoroughly wet bird is now stood out of the bath and the squeezed-out sponge used to mop off as much moisture as possible. The first large towel is wrapped round the fowl and additional patting and mopping takes place.

## PREPARING LEGS AND FEET

The second towel is then wrapped around the bird and the operator sits with it across his knees. The fowl is laid on its side its legs being forward either to his right or left hand, according to the way he usually performs manual work.

He now takes a sharpened stick and gently inserts it under any scale in which dirt has lodged. By careful manipulation (which soon becomes easy, by practice) each rim of dirt can be removed and the bird shown with faultless legs. This is somewhat tedious but exhibitors gain their rewards by taking this sort of care.

## DRYING BIRDS

An ordinary show hamper should be littered with clean straw, which has advantages over other litter. It will allow droppings to fall through; fowls cannot scratch in long straw which has been arranged as a "bed" within the space afforded by a hamper.

There should be a steady source of clean heat available. If an open, hard-fuel fire is still in use, it should have been made up before the washing process began and be burning brightly when it is over.

The washed bird, its legs manicured, is placed in the prepared hamper and placed before the fire. It should be dried reasonably quickly but not be scorched. If the source of heat is too fierce, plumage will dry out rather brittle and curled.

When it is partially dry, a soft feathered bird with copious fluff may be taken out and its fluffy plumage well rubbed with a dry towel. Otherwise, leave (overnight is usually convenient) until dry and remove to its showpen the following morning. A first feed of bread and milk will be easily digested and help restore natural lustre to the plumage.

The skilled operator will have his own timetable for this operation. The newer exhibitor should allow three days from washing to exhibition, to allow his birds to "web out" and recover natural appearance of plumage.

## COMMENT ON METHOD

It is understood that fanciers with enquiring minds will devise their own methods of washing a bird for show. The method given is a foolproof and efficient way which can be used by those who do not have electrical gadgets available to them. It can be used as the "norm" and local adjustments made, as wanted.

There are many washing agents on the market today and there could be nothing against them if efficient. I suggest it would be wise to try out any detergents which might be favoured in the household on some less valuable birds in need of a bath, to test reaction.

It needs little imagination on the part of those fitted with mechanical knowledge to devise electrically heated "drying boxes" in which birds can be quickly and evenly dried after their full wash. Others may choose to employ hair dryers, fan heaters and so on to give, at least, the initial drying.

Whatever is used, the idea must be to promote steady, even warmth for some time rather than fierce heat for a short time.

Figure 13. Light Sussex Cock (Reserve Champion National Show — Hall & Sons)

# CHAPTER 10

## KNOW YOUR STANDARD

### BRITISH POULTRY STANDARDS

THE FIRST STANDARDS were the outcome of expression of opinion by men who were judging all fowls at early shows. They described the various breeds as they thought they ough to be but, being heir to the human failings which beset us all their work was not perfect. Nor had it the benefit of good illustration.

Today, there is no excuse for exhibitors not knowing what the written word is intended to convey. The book, *British Poultry Standards*, contains, in addition to detailed descriptions, re-touched photographs of leading winners considered to conform to Standard requirements. From them can be gained a very good idea of what sort of bird is needed to win.

Additionally, there are several pages in colour of specimen feathers taken from birds which were excellent and others which had some prevalent fault. Thus, what is desirable and what to avoid can be assessed in all the usual plumage patterns.

The poultry fancy owes a great debt to the late C.G. May, former Editor of *Poultry World,* who devoted many, many hours to the task of editing Standards issued by specialist breed clubs into one, easily assimilated form. That he was assisted by a committee of advisers whose knowledge was freely placed at his disposal did not lessen his editorial task at a time when other aspects of poultry-keeping occupied him and fancy poultry were being displaced by myriads of commercial fowls.

If no other tribute is recorded to George May, who championed show poultry in the face of some pretty fierce opposition, let me (who rendered as much assistance in revising the Standards as my professional duties permitted) write these paragraphs to remind fanciers of the man who master-minded *British Poultry Standards* as they exist today.

While Standards are not absolute they do give excellent guidance and set down, in their tables of points, which are the most important features of any breed as well as all the minor features which go to make the perfect bird.

# KNOW YOUR STANDARD

It will be advantageous to look closely at Standards for all breeds and come to a conclusion as to what are their principal requirements. At the same time, such examination may help to dispel some common fallacies as to whether breeds ought to be judged mainly on shape, or colour, or headpoints.

If we allow that any Standard giving 35 points or more for **type** and **size** indicates a breed or variety in which shape is the main requirement; 35 points or more for **colour** and/or **markings**, plus **legs**, is a "colour" breed and the same number for **head** including **beak** must be regarded as a "head" breed, we will have achieved some degree of consistency when reading the Standards.

It is easier, perhaps, to memorise the *Head* and *Colour* breeds and know that all those not included on these lists should be first selected for **type**.

## HEAD BREEDS

The *Head* breeds are few and with the exception of the Minorca do not include any other of those usually thought to be "lobe and comb" breeds.

The list comprises:—

**Large Fowl**

Houdan — crested and muffled with distinctive comb.
Poland — crested with some varieties also muffled.
Sultan — crested, bearded and muffled.
Redcap — excessive development of fully double rose comb.
Minorca — precise requirements face, comb and lobes.
Spanish — excessive development of lobes and face.

## COLOUR BREEDS

There are rather more "colour" breeds in which this point is most important and one or two of them are excessively rated for perfection in colour and markings. In these the points allocated for type are so low as to be absurd.

In others, which only marginally qualify to be included in this list, the number of points for **Colour** and **Legs** outweighs those for **Type** and **Size** by the merest trifle and the breed may be regarded as balanced between **Type** and **Colour**. The Barnevelder is a good example.

A few breeds can claim to have paid regard to all requirements when their Standards were compiled. Points are fairly evenly divided between **Type, Colour** and **Head** with **Colour** just having two or three more points to qualify for inclusion in this list. An outstanding example is the Leghorn, so often and incorrectly regarded as a "comb and lobe" breed and so considered when judging takes place. By its Standard it should first be assessed for Colour, then Type and, finally Head.

Another popular breed must be judged according to variety. It is no use expecting all Wyandottes to approximate to the White and judging them, firstly, for type. The Standards clearly lay down that marked and coloured varieties should gain more points under those headings than they do for shape. In fact, some of the Standards (e.g. Blue Laced) do not mention **Type** at all.

"Colour" Breeds are: —

| **Large Fowl** | Hamburgh |
| Ancona | Leghorn |
| Andalusian | Old English Pheasant Fowl |
| Barnevelder | Plymouth Rock |
| Brahma | Scots Grey |
| Campine | Wyandotte (some varieties) |

All other breeds give more points to **Type** than other features but there are one or two peculiarities which deserve attention.

In Frizzles there are 30 points for curl of feather; Modern Game, Sumatra Game and Welsummers give as many points to **Colour** as **Type**; North Holland Blues have 40 points for **Utility Merits** which do not fall within any of the three groups previously mentioned; and Yokohamas have 45 points for **Plumage.**

Although nearly all breeds can be accommodated in one of the three groups shown above and the relative importance of their main features easily memorised by referring to the lists it must be appreciated that every breed not excepting Hamburghs which give only 10 points for Type, Style and **Condition** and some Laced Wyandottes which give none should have distinctive shape (**Type**), heads and other details without which they cannot be claimed to represent their breed.

These are described in similar manner in each Standard and conscious effort ought to be made to select birds approximating to their descriptions regardless of the major importance of other features.

Thus, to return to our example of Blue Laced Wyandottes, any exhibit ought to show the prime requirements of a Wyandotte as described in the Standard under **Type** – body short and deep with well rounded sides etc., etc.

It would only be if such a shapely bird were absolutely deficient in clarity of ground colour and definition of lacing that it could lose to another with square shoulders and a long, flat back, but having the better markings.

In the light of what has been written it ought to be realised that a competent judge will assess any exhibit as a whole. He will not try to evaluate the points for each feature but will use his experience and offset some undoubted excellence against a point of demerit in some other part of the bird and.

One ought, therefore, always strive to present a "balanced" exhibit as being likeliest to attract most judges but, at the same time, throw emphasis on the prime feature of the breed concerned whether it be **Type, Colour** or **Head.**

## BANTAMS

Miniatures of large breeds should be considered in the same way as their large counterparts but a few bantams need to be assessed in their own right as true dwarfs.

As it happens some of them (e.g.; Barbu d'Uccles) have fairly complicated Standards with no less than twelve different features named as being worthy of a number of points. It is important for exhibitors and judges alike to pay careful regard to the Standards for the few breeds concerned as all of them vary considerably when compared with another.

The Bantam breeds are:–

| | |
|---|---|
| Barbu d'Anvers | Japanese |
| Barbu d'Uccle | Nankin |
| Pekin | Rosecomb |
| Frizzle | Sebright |

The Japanese is outstandingly a **Type** breed having 70 points for **Type** and **Size** but none for **Head**. Yet this feature is important and the single comb is precisely defined. The Sebright, often said to be a **Type** breed is, however, a "Colour and Markings" subject with half the total points for these features.

These examples only underline the importance of a fair-minded approach to the selection of birds for exhibition which will result in a balanced lot for a judge to choose from, at any show.

## WHAT SORT WINS

In addition, there must be taken into account what sort of bird usually wins in the breed under review. In some the Standards are requirements which were absolutely accurate for the birds which existed when the written word was first published.

During the evolution of the breed, selection for certain points of merit has been intensified to such an extent that the present-day winner and the original fowl have not a lot in common except name.

**Examples**

Probably to the indignation of its chief supporters, let us glance at the Standard for Indian Game in certain vital respects. Carriage, one would think, gives a clue to the general character of the fowl. The Standard says, "A powerful and broad bird very active, sprightly and vigorous". What wins in the showpen is a very broad bird, stodgy and heavy of foot, often wheezing as it stands there and certainly panting when one picks it up to examine it during judging.

In Type, it says, "Elegance is required with substance" but the meaning of elegance is "grace, refinement" – not always much in evidence in the heavyweights. Legs and Feet are wanted thus: "The length of shank must be sufficient to give the bird a 'gamey' appearance". In fact, the frontal of a winning Indian cock is as nearly square as fowls can be bred and shanks are short.

Not very long ago I had to make enquiries on behalf of a foreign buyer and was unable to get one promise of hatching eggs in season, the general plea being that breeders could no longer rely on the percentage of fertility likely to be found in their stock, all of which were bred to modern requirements. *This would appear to be a case where fashion has departed too far from the written Standard!*

## Minorcas

But, what would happen if one exhibited a Minorca with earlobes not exceeding "2¾ inches deep and 1½ inches at its widest part at the top, tapering as the Valencia almond in shape". Would those lobes be considered big enough? Would the true almond shape be preferred to the oval?

The answer would certainly be "no" for any of the important shows!

## SYSTEMATIC SCRUTINY

How to know that a potential winner is in hand is something which follows careful and systematic scrutiny. Look first at the head, since this is what the judge sees as he approaches the pen and is most readily assessed by him. See that the comb is right in shape, size and texture. In some cases, e.g. Brown-red Modern Game and Silkies, see that unusual colour is correct, too.

Immediately check eye colour. If the Standard says eyes are grey or hazel for some colours of plumage but black or brown in others (as it does for Faverolles) then follow the Standard. Red for any of them just will not do even though the fault be common enough in many birds.

At the same time, look at lobes and faces. All are described in their respective Standards and should be correct in form, shape and colour.

Pass from the head down the neck hackle, checking that feathers are of the proper shape, colour, markings. Continue down the back to the saddle or cushion, parting the feathers at the base of the tail proper to see that the sickle feathers (in males) are properly made, developed and sound in colour.

Put the hand in the back of the main tail and spread the feathers outwards and upwards by applying a little pressure with the flat hand. It should be possible to check that the full complement of fourteen tail feathers is there. If this is not checked at home, the judge will soon downpoint a bird not complete in this important detail, when he checks at a show.

Spread each wing in turn. See there are no gaps anywhere and that the primaries close nicely under the secondary feathers. Look at colour and markings in breeds where these exist.

Scrutinise thighs, legs and feet. Check that they are soundly made and colour is right. In some breeds — like Australorps — take a look at the soles of the feet, ensuring that colour is according to Standard and that no yellow pigment has crept in by negligent selection in the breeding pen.

## CHECK TOES

In some breeds formation of toes, with particular reference to a firm, well-spread back toe (particularly important in five-toed breeds) should always be checked.

With the fowl facing the operator, each hand should be passed round the lower thigh and the wing tips taken down and restrained by each thumb. The bird is then quickly lifted and tilted head down.

Its claws will be fully unclenched and crooked toes or badly set-on back toes (especially those with the fault known as "duck-footed" when the back toe roughly follows the same line as a side toe) will show up very clearly.

## GENERAL EXAMINATION

While this general examination is going on, the breeder should be applying his knowledge of Standard requirements automatically and without conscious reference to the precise points of head, feet, shape, plumage, colour, markings, etc., which are laid down.

First, he must know his Standard. Second, he must select in accordance with it. Third, he can check two or more birds side-by-side with detailed reference to the points they may score at a show — and so select the best of what he has to appear against all comers at the show of his choice.

The judge's verdict will tell him whether his knowledge and his method of selection have been good enough, on this occasion.

# CHAPTER 11

## HOW THE JUDGE WORKS

### KNOWING THE APPROACH

A LOOK INSIDE the mind of a judge ought to help exhibitors to know what obvious snags to avoid when showing. Because they are deeply wrapped up in their own problems, breeders tend to think any judge must see things from the same standpoint. In the time at his disposal a judge cannot allow some minor point, which may be difficult of production, to be of more Standard value than some other feature which this breeder takes for granted because he has it firmly implanted in his stock.

Immediately, the exhibitor disagrees with the judge's interpretation.

The exhibitor who "thinks it out" before he enters some particular specimen under a particular judge ought to know from past experience what that judge thinks and he should show accordingly. "Horses for courses" if you like – but a very effective way of prizewinning.

## JUDGING METHOD

Repeated analysis of my own efforts at judging, spread over the years at large shows and small, home and abroad, show that first assessment, making notes in judging book, final comparisons and ultimate awarding of prizes takes an average of one minute per bird.

Much depends on the number of birds in a class, quality of exhibits, whether all of one variety or mixed colours and so on. But the average stands.

In general, what happens is this, and I give my own personal experience. The judge looks at the heading for the class in his judging book. He checks what he has to assess and notes the number of prizes to be awarded.

He walks down the pens and records any that are empty, putting a tick against birds which appear to be outstanding because of type and headpoints and/or condition – all of which can be seen at a glance!

He then goes back to the first pen in the class and with his steward to assist in opening and closing pen doors and removing each bird from its pen, he takes the exhibits in hand and subjects them to a rapid but close scrutiny.

My own method is to hold the bird in the left hand, one finger along the keel so that the fowl can "ride" comfortably. The thumb on one side and fingers on the other restrain the bird's legs and wings. With the right hand I hold the different parts under examination starting with comb, lobes, wattles, eyes and face. At this examination both Standard points and facial condition are noted.

The right hand is then passed down the neck hackle and, if markings are involved or undercolour is critical, feathers are parted and an examination made at several points in the neck, finishing with the lower hackle feathers.

The hand then passes over the back, down to the saddle in males, cushion in females. Any physical fault is noted and colour, markings and other features are examined. Then to the root of the tail for an inspection of colour and sound condition, looking especially for anything which might have been done with the intention to deceive. A check on the number of main tail feathers and quickly back to the wings, spreading each in turn. Finally, a look at the breast feathering and under-parts followed by an assessment of feet and legs, as described earlier in this book.

All this is within, say, 20 seconds and one must know how the bird accords with its Standard. A quick scribble in the judging book and a tick for something sound but not of first quality, with a cross tick for any of those first noted which have turned out to be satisfactory on examination.

If three out of ten have gained a cross tick they will have done well, and can be compared, side by side if necessary for first, second and third prizes. Others will be given cards of commendation when the salient features noted in the judging book can be consulted. Thus, "faulty comb" in most breeds would result in a lower placing than "slightly weak undercolour". The reasons are obvious: the comb is there for all to see and is something which can soon be inbred. Undercolour is a hidden fault and can be corrected by careful selection in the breeding pen.

*Experience has taught that while the approach is modified as one goes to different sections of the show it must be based*

72

*on knowledge of the Standards for the breeds concerned.*
I do not recall that I have ever had consciously to shift my
ground even when acting as sole judge and having three or
four hours work ahead of me. But all the warning lights have,
apparently, gone on in my mind as I have walked towards
some section of classes and I have been aware of what main
faults and weaknesses might be present and what values
attached to them, before I have handled one of the exhibits.

## EXAMPLE – HARD FEATHER BREEDS

In hard feather, one knows that large **Old English Game**
must be sound, fit and active. That muscles must be firm and
weight reduced to the minimum permissible to give good show
condition.

The first walk down the pens and those initial ticks will be
awarded to cocks which are radiantly fit and stand with hocks
properly angled. Some may be large, show cocks; some may
be smaller but proud and agile. If two sorts are found the
decision must be quickly taken which are to be preferred,
bearing in mind that this is a show where competition is on
appearance only and all the pen-side talk of what the little
beggar can do must be discounted. In hens, those which are
short and well cut up behind will handle better than others
which are, obviously, in lay and allowances must be made as
one works.

Legs and feet will be of prime importance; examination of
heels will be critical. Wings must be long enough to protect
thighs and this will be tested. Game cocks will be handled
with head away from the judge so that the way the birds
"ride" in both hands can be tested. They will be returned to
their pens with a little throw so that the manner in which
they assume their stance can easily be seen.

Colour will be of less importance than most other breeds
but should accord with whatever it purports to be. Condition
is essential and birds must be clean and well presented; their
heads and legs having been groomed. I have been severely
criticised for leaving out a thoroughly good Pile cock which
was dirty in plumage and filthy in head and legs, the owner
disregarding entirely that he had brought **the bird to an**
exhibition and not a cockpit. **As I could not reasonably**
compare the bird, **point by point, with other entries because**

Figure 14. Pile Old English Game bantam male as currently exhibited. (Owned by Mr. Sam Lean)

of its dirtiness I felt I was right in passing it by.

Modern Game, rare though they are, must pass the same tests as they were (originally) a selection from the fighting fowl. Malays should always be checked for "cow hocks" deriving from a degree of leg weakness and eyes of the wrong colour. Indian Game are not fitted for battle and more consideration is given to their colour and markings, allied with good condition. This is, essentially, a type breed and no perfection in colour can put a poorly shaped Indian into the cards. As one approaches the classes for females one recollects that the top of the breast is not double laced like the remainder but wholly black; a stumbling block for both breeder and judge in some cases.

When turning to Old English Game bantams one moves the viewpoint a little, realising that the miniatures are not built on the same lines as the large breed.

One accepts that a certain style of bird is generally accepted as Old English Game and makes selections accordingly. Strict application of the written Standard would result in many bantams being passed by. In Figure 10 the Old English Game Pile cockerel, a consistent winner, would have been "passed" if the strict Standards were followed. For example, the Oxford Standard on which the Poultry Club Standard is based calls for a large tail and strong wings which cover the thighs. No judge these days would expect to see a large tail, although, at the same time, if a bird lacks tail to a marked degree he should be penalised.

The tests made amongst large Game for activity should, in my view, still be made and feet (especially back toes in males) carefully scrutinised. Colour is more important than in large fowl and frequently the "pretty" pullet will win top honours.

Modern Game bantams are now, essentially, a colour breed with long limbs and none of them have the hardness and vigour which ought to be theirs. Sound feet and tightly carried wings are two points the knowledgeable judge will look for. He will also be impressed if the thighs are longer than the shanks and by some healthy glow in headpoints.

Indian Game bantams are often better, point for point, than the large breed but the cockerels are frequently too black in plumage and many of the females too feathery behind the thighs. Most judges are on the alert for tell-tale signs of "improvement" here.

## SOFT FEATHER – HEAVY BREEDS

Soft feathered breeds are so diverse that one re-orientates as the class heading is read. In other words, *general* rules have to be modified for each breed.

Large, heavy breeds must be just that – large and heavy! I have taken some Sussex out of their pens and found them with razor-edged breastbones devoid of that flesh which makes a good table fowl. No matter how marked, they have been returned with scant ceremony as not typical of the breed.

Most soft feathered heavy breeds are "type" fowls and if they are the wrong shape, especially if they strike the judge as wrong when he first walks down the pens, they cannot get into the top awards. My experience is that first impressions for shape and style are almost invariably right in the end.

Each bird must be handled for plumage, colour and markings and it goes without saying that hidden points in some breeds, e.g., Rhode Island Reds, can be important.

Faulty combs may not lose so many points that birds cannot have a prize, but if the choice must be made between two of almost equal merit, the better combed bird will usually win.

One's warning signals flash on as one approaches **Barred Rocks,** for split wings: **Buff Rocks,** weak undercolour or stained tails: **Light Sussex,** run-through black striping in hackles and white in earlobes: **White Sussex,** not typical in shape: **Orpingtons,** too much feather and not enough body: **Wyandottes,** too much fluff above the hocks and lack of full complement in tails: **Australorps,** eyes and soles of feet of wrong colouring: **Dorkings,** below Standard size and faulty back toes. These examples will demonstrate how the judge's mind reacts to the naming of a breed. His experience warns him that prevalent faults will also be present in the exhibits of the day and he must be on guard against too much toleration.

The same points are evident in bantams of these breeds. They also have some inbred defects of their own like white in earlobe in some varieties of **Wyandottes** or red in shanks of **Sussex;** willow legs in **Buff Rocks** and poor comb formation in **Rhode Islands Reds.**

## SOFT FEATHER – LIGHT BREEDS

Turning to light breeds, with their precisely formed combs and white earlobes, one notes those which are white in face at early maturity and which can only get worse as time goes on. They are downpointed. So also are the birds which have some greivous fault in comb formation which they cannot hide.

Rosecombed breeds, like **Hamburghs**, are carefully looked over for evidence of trimming combs to get them to better shape and size than they originally were. Light breed females, with very large combs, are checked for blindness on the side to which the comb falls. Lobes are examined for hollows and thin texture; for blisters and discolouration, as well as for shape.

## SOFT FEATHER – ORNAMENTAL BANTAMS

A group which stands alone consists of **Ornamental** bantams. When I nominated a **Poland** for best in show and offered it to a Game judge to handle, he refused, saying, "That bird is like a handful of butterflies. Tell me if it's a real good 'un'.

One gathers from this that some judges are prepared to allow these birds to be shown with less bodily condition than breeds of more ordinary make and style. While I do not subscribe to this view altogether I would say that the points of ornamentation are usually so difficult to get and maintain that Ornamental bantams are more widely kept in sheltered pens and cannot be as fit as many others.

When one considers their crests, muffled faces, whiskers, leg feather, curled plumage, extravagant combs and lobes it becomes apparent that these points of beauty must take precedence over most other features and judges approach these delicate beauties with rare and delicate understanding.

This does not mean that they can be positively unfit and stand in a dejected, sickly manner. But they will rarely be as radiant as the Game birds which my co-judge had been handling all the morning before he was offered my "handful of butterflies".

Some physical faults are liable to crop up at random in any breed. A judge is on his guard all the time and readily notes exhibits which may have roach backs (rounded instead of flat); wry tails (permanently carried to one side); duck foot (with the back toe carried to one side) and so on.

He is aware that roach back, for instance, is more readily discernible in a light breed cockerel than a heavy breed pullet but knows that the fault is just as bad in the one as the other.

A competent judge, therefore, has mentally tabulated those physical faults which are general and is prepared to downpoint an exhibit or put it out of the reckoning for a prize altogether if it has what the Standards describe as a **Serious Defect**.

In order the better to convey what the likeliest faults look like, some sketches have been prepared. When glancing at them it should be appreciated that the faults have been intensified and it is highly unlikely that such defects will be encountered to this degree in birds seen at shows.

But the faults may occur, in lesser degree, and exhibitors must not grumble if they regard "just a little sidesprig" as permissible in comb (because their strain has it!) while the judge regards it as a Serious Defect because it is so listed in many Standards.

In any case, breeders should make a serious effort to exclude from their breeding pens any birds with such faults as they are hereditary and can only become intensified as the years go by.

## TYPE FEATURES

We now turn to some popular misconceptions about similarities and differences between breeds. In some cases, because of a common factor which appears to be the same (e.g; single combs and white earlobes) breeds are "paired" in the minds of many exhibitors and some judges and considered from exactly the same standpoint.

That this is an error can readily be found if the Standards are wholly and carefully read. It is not difficult to pick out a phrase from its context and find precisely the same words in the Standard for another breed. This may lead some people to suppose that the breeds are, therefore, identical.

But – and it is a very big **BUT** – the rest of the description in the two Standards will have points of variance and those relating to **Type** are of critical importance.

In order to throw emphasis on the points of breeds popularly "paired" by unthinking fanciers I have prepared some silhouettes which show **Type** as described in the Standards, but not necessarily as currently exhibited.

To assist in concentration on this salient feature the heads and shanks are not shown and details of lobes, wing carriage, etc, are, of course, "blacked out".

Although differences in some of the examples are not very great they do exist and, once appreciated, will help to guide exhibitors and judges alike in their appraisals of a number of our more popular breeds.

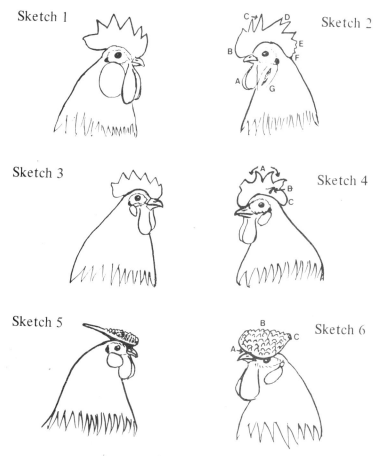

Figure 15. Sketches of Heads

## KEY TO SKETCHES OF HEADS

**Sketch**

1. Example of good, large single combed cockerel having wide serrations, open lobes and well developed wattles.
2. Many faults exemplified are:
   A undersized wattles;
   B front of comb overhangs point of beak;
   C two narrow serrations known as "pencilled spikes";
   D fish-tailed serration;
   E poor finish to blade of comb;
   F comb presses on neck hackle;
   G hollow lobe.
3. Neat head on a heavy breed male.
4. A Irregularly shaped serrations; B side spring; C "plain" blade.
5. Neat rose comb of Hamburgh type with leader carried well out at rear.
6. Over developed rose comb of Redcap type:
   A comb pressing down at one side almost obscuring eye;
   B coarse, open "work" on top of comb;
   C ingrown leader;

## KEY TO SKETCHES OF BODIES (Figure 12)

**Sketch**

1. Squirrel tail in which the tail is carried too far forward making an acute angle with the line of the back.
2. Looking down over the back it is seen that the tail is carried to one side, instead of being straight out in line with the neck.
   This is an example of "wry" tail.
3. Cutaway front with insufficient development of breast often found in "lanky", slow-growing, heavy breed cockerels.
4. Roach back where the skeleton of the bird has a convex curve over the back, instead of it being flat.

5.  Straight hocks in any breed but particularly bad in Old English Game where there must be an angle at the junction between the shanks and thighs.

6.  Any Modern Game with shanks longer than the thighs is said to be "stork-legged". Lift and reach ought to be achieved by having the thighs slightly longer.

Sketch 1

Sketch 2

Sketch 3

Sketch 4

Sketch 5

Sketch 6

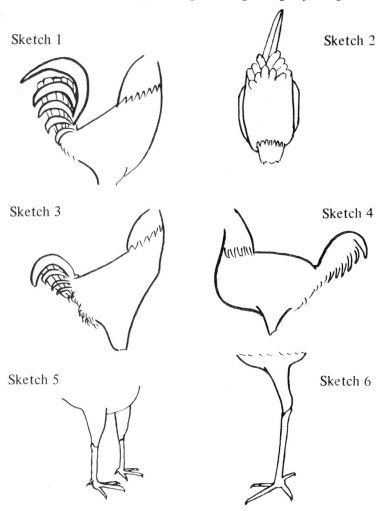

Figure 16. Common Faults

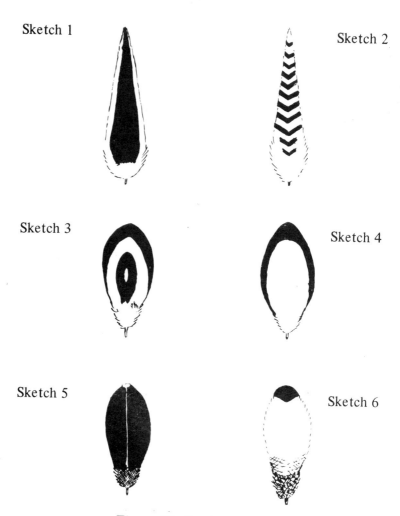

Sketch 1

Sketch 2

Sketch 3

Sketch 4

Sketch 5

Sketch 6

Figure 17. Feather Faults.

## KEY TO SKETCHES OF FEATHERS

Feather markings must comply with the **Standards** and the following notes show common **faults** which occur.
Sketch
1.  Instead of the black centre stripe being completely contained by the white margin it "runs through" to the end of the feather which also has a fine black

outer edging which ought not to be there. This fault is known, in this context, as "double lacing".

2. Faults in this barred feather include a white tip, which ought to be black; narrow V-shaped barring instead of being straight across the feather; irregular portions of ground colour instead of being equal with the black bars.

3. Double laced breed which is far too heavy in black. The outer lacing is too thick at the end and the centre lacing has far too little ground colour displayed within it.

4. Feather from a laced variety which is almost crescentic at the tip and rather too heavy down the sides of the feather.

5. Small, irregular white tip instead of a well-defined, clean end to the feather of a tipped or mottled variety. The feather also shows a light shaft which ought to be solid black; a fault known as "shaftiness".

6. Hamburghs should have large blobs on the end of their feathers but many are found with the prevailing fault of V-shaped tippings and too much undercolour.

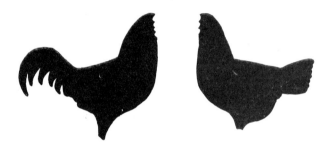

**Figure 18. Leghorn Male (left) and Ancona Female**

Confusion between the Leghorn (male, left) and Ancona (female, right) probably arises because both breeds originally came from the same general area and both have single combs and white earlobes. The Leghorn has a long, flat back, sloping to the tail which is moderately full and carried at an angle of 45 deg. from the line of the back. This Standard feature is not often met and, when it is, is likely to be largely disregarded as not representing the proper tail carriage for the breed. Shanks in the Leghorn are moderately long.

While the Ancona has a back of good length the breed is specifically demanded to have a compact body which sits well down on the thighs which are not wanted to be much seen. The tail is full and carried well out but not, as so often met within the showpen, carried whipped.

**Figure 19. Andalusian Male (left) and Minorca Female**

In some cases distinction between the Andalusian (male, left) and Minorca (female, right) is not as marked as it ought to be, simply because the breeds have been crossed to gain points other than Type. A long body, with a full, round breast ought to characterise the Andalusian whose tail must be large and flowing and carried fairly high. The legs are long. In the Minorca the body ought to be square and compact with a full breast, not long and racy, as so often shown. Her tail is full and carried well back while stout thighs complete the proper proportions of this heavyweight light breed.

85

Figure 20. Sussex Male (left) and Dorking Female

Because it is highly probable that the Dorking (female, right) lent some of its virtues to the basic processes which made the Sussex (male, left) there is bound to be some similarity especially in white skins and fineness of flesh. Due to the fact that the Sussex also had a large infusion of Asiatic blood, external characteristics differ. The Sussex male shows a flat back of reasonable length and a heavy body with square breast. The moderately sized tail is carried at an angle of 45 deg. while thighs are short and stout. An essential difference, shown by the Dorking, is that it has a long, deep, rectangular shaped body while its large thighs are almost hidden by body feathering. The tail should be full and carried well out.

**Figure 21. Modern Game Male (left) and Old English Game Female**

Modern Game (male, left) derived from Old English Game (female, right) when shows became well established. There is similarity in that both ought to have a short, flat back. The Modern Game must have long and well rounded thighs and a closely whipped tail, carried just above the level of the body. The Old English hen is fuller in the breast and thighs are short and form an angle with the shanks. The tail is large and fan shaped and ought to be carried well up. Large Old English game males achieve large tails, but in bantams it is more usual to find show specimens with rather whipped tails.

Figure 22. Brahma Male (left) and Cochin Female

Both large, both Asiatic in origin and both feathered legged, the Brahma (male, left) and Cochin (female, right) have all too often been confused as to Type. There should, however, be considerable distinction between the breeds. The Brahma has a broad, square and deep body and a short back, with saddle rising halfway between the hackle and the tail. The tail is of medium length, and carried nearly upright. The breast is full and the bird has a horizontal keel. Thighs are large. Plumage is reasonably close.

The Cochin has a large, deep body and the breast must come as low down as possible. The back is short and the cushion convex, the tail being carried almost flat. (A common fault is the cushion concave and the tail rather upright.) The thighs are large but completely covered with feathers.

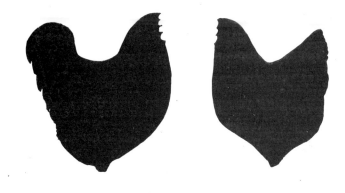

**Figure 23.** Orpington Male (left) and Wyandotte Female

Because they, too, have "borrowed" from each other in the past, there is often too much similarity between Orpingtons (male, left) and Wyandottes (female, right). They should be quite distinct in **Type**, especially style and carriage of the tail. The Orpington has a deep, cobby body with a rather short, curved back with concave outline. The breast is deep and well rounded and the tail which is rather short and flowing ought to be carried high. Legs are short and strong, the thighs almost hidden by body feathers. In the Wyandotte the body is also short and deep, with full and round breast. Thighs are of medium length and, since plumage is required to be fairly close and silky, there is no reference to the thighs being hidden by body feather: which should not be the case. The medium sized tail is full but spread at the base, and this point is not as strongly in evidence as one might wish.

**Figure 24. Plymouth Rock Male (left) and
Rhode Island Red Female**

Plymouth Rocks (male, left) and Rhode Island Reds (female, right) both came from the United States of America. Both have yellow skins and both are good, all-round breeds. There, the main common factors should remain. The Rock is a large, deep, compact breed with well rounded breast. Everything about it should comply with the key-word "moderation" and all parts of the body should be gently rounded. The medium sized tail rises slightly from the back and should not be fan shaped. Thighs are large and of medium length. The Rhode Island Red should have a long body of fair depth, giving an overall "oblong" look. The long back is nearly horizontal and the breast ought to be carried nearly perpendicular with the base of the beak. A medium length tail, with feathers well spread, ought to be carried well out to increase the apparent length of the back. Thighs are large and of medium length.

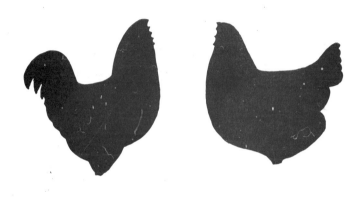

**Figure 25. Marans Male (left) and North Holland Blue Female**

Because they are both white skinned and cuckoo coloured many people confuse the Marans (male, left) with the North Holland Blue (female, right). In the Marans the body is of medium length but with good width and depth and the tail is carried high. Legs are of medium length and thighs well fleshed. The North Holland Blue, on the other hand, has a longish back which is carried horizontal and the tail is broad and well spread. The breast must be rounded and well developed and the keel long. Thighs are medium in size.

91

# FAULTS

Possibly the most controversial area in showing is the extent to which birds should be penalised when faults are found by the judge. How often have fanciers heard the statement: "This bird should not have been given a prize because he is duck footed"! The Game Fancier looks at his young stock, intent on culling if this dreaded fault should appear.

The British, American and other *Standards* specify faults which should be penalised such as:

1. Not conforming to breed characteristics.

2. Signs of faking.

3. Suffering from disease or obviously out of condition.

4. Defects:

    (a)   not correct height;

    (b)   wrong colour;

    (c)   faulty feather conformation

    (d)   faulty legs such as five toes when four is normal or duck footed.

The British *Standards* list 'Serious Defects' and 'Defects' which should presumably be interpreted as 'Disqualifications' or 'Penalties'. The American *Standards* are more positive and state the disqualifications under a separate heading.

## EXAMPLES OF DEFECTS

Figure 26. Duck Footed

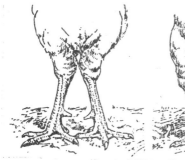

Figure 27. Knock-Kneed                    Bow Legged
(Faulty Legs)

Figure 28. Fish-tailed Comb          Twisted Comb
(Faulty Comb)
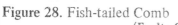
Other similar defects to be penalised

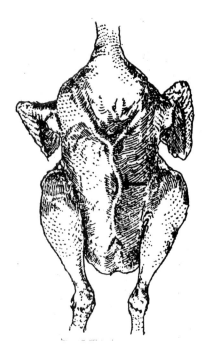

**Figure 29.** Twisted Keel

**Figure 30.** Faulty Crest

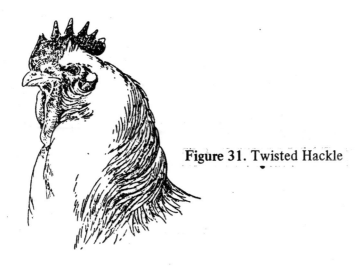

**Figure 31.** Twisted Hackle

## CONCLUSION

In the foregoing I have tried to show what is in a judge's mind as he approaches different sections of a show and different classes within a section to carry out his sole task of selecting for prizes those birds which are nearest to the accepted *Standard*.

If the Exhibitor will try to adopt a similar standpoint and go through the same drill before he selects his birds for show, he might win more consistently than he sometimes does when blinded by one feature which he considers important but which the Standard and the judge together do

95

not rate very highly.

Being human, judges must make mistakes sometimes. At the best, what they offer is informed opinion on the merits of exhibits. In the case of experienced adjudicators this coincides with what other judges have offered to a remarkable degree and must be the yardstick by which exhibition fowls are measured.

# CHAPTER 12

## SHOWDAY AND AFTERCARE

BEFORE SHOWDAY DAWNS the fancier has selected his best specimens and has conditioned them with the definite date in view. He must, also, have made his entries to the show secretary.

## SHOW ENTRIES

The name and address of the secretary of a show has been noted from an advertisement in the fancy press, usually *Poultry World* or *Fur and Feather*. A schedule of classes and prizes has been obtained and the rate of entry fee and closing date for entries noted.

The classification is scrutinised to find the most suitable classes for the selected birds. Care is taken over ages and varieties in those breeds where classes are given for both adult and young stock and for different colours of the same breed.

The society's entry form, sent out with schedules, is completed and returned together with appropriate entry fees before the date shown for closing of entries.

If the show authorities send out numbered leg rings they should be placed on a shank, one to each fowl, according to entries. If pen labels are sent these will show the class and pen number of each entry. Labels for rail transit are usually sent on request; the majority of exhibitors and their birds now travel by road vehicles of one sort or another and a list of their pen number suffices.

## AT THE SHOW

Equipment needed for successful showing comprises:
1. A large duster.
2. Clean hand towel.
3. Small sponge.
4. Bottle of head dressing.
5. Poultry food.

If the exhibitor has a method which he always practises he will get through the finicky and slightly tedious business of packing exhibits at home; unpacking and penning at the show better than the man who is always rushing around in panic.

## SUGGESTED ROUTINE

After a very small, early morning feed of corn, each show entry is taken from its pen at home and placed gently in a section of an exhibition hamper which has previously been labelled and had clean litter placed on the floor.

Not forgetting the equipment, mentioned above, probably packed in a polythene bag overnight, the owner gets on to the road early so as to be at the show with enough time to do what's necessary without undue haste.

Placing his hampers where they will not be in the way of other keen exhibitors, he goes to each of the numbered pens which his own exhibits will occupy. Regardless of how clean they may seem to be, he wipes the galvanised partitions with a large clean duster. The exhibitor who has never done this before will be surprised at the state of the duster after wiping. At the least, it will have a film of dust. At the worst, there will be dried mud from some other show where tents may have been taken down in a rainstorm.

The first bird is now taken from the basket and stood on the lid. The towel is draped over its back and down its sides. It is lifted and held, headfirst, under the left arm. The small sponge is moistened with head dressing and the comb, face, wattles and earlobes are gently wiped over. A corner of the towel gives a final, dry wiping.

The legs are cleaned from any adhering droppings which may have been voided on the journey.

The bird is carried, with the towel still round it, to the appropriate pen. It is placed, headfirst, in the pen and its plumage smoothed by hand. The bird is then "set up" as though at home in the training pen.

If necessary, it is given just a little of some favourite dry food which has been brought along, to settle it in.

*Everything possible has now been done to ensure a fit, clean bird, in top condition, for the judge's inspection and appraisal.*

The other birds in the team are dealt with in the same way. All is done in due order and by the time the chief steward calls "All exhibitors outside please" the last bird hould have been put down as tidily as the others. The rest is in the hands (and mind) of the judge, but birds onditioned and presented as described in this book will never e a reproach to their owner. If they have as much Standard ierit as they have show bloom they could well be champions.

## HEAD DRESSING

The sole purpose of head dressing is to freshen the head-oints of a bird which is already fit. It is not a magic potion ιhich can work miracles for unfit birds. It is only used after irds have undertaken a journey or when they are basketed ᴐ be sent to some classic show where all the birds pass arough the hands of the appointed stewards.

A few years ago I was jointly responsible for the champion-iip awards at the Royal Dairy Show. After they had been iade an exhibitor made himself known and asked what I iought of the condition of his ornamental bantam which 'as runner-up to the champion.

When I answered that it was very good for such a breed he raised the head dressing, which I had previously publicised, id said it had "made all the difference" to his showing as ᴐmpared with results he had previously obtained.

I give the formula here for the dressing to be made up y a chemist:

**Formula for Head Dressing**

2 oz. spirits of wine.
1 oz. camphorated oil.
1 oz. glycerine.
¼ oz. citric acid.

Mix well. Apply sparingly, and only when required.

## AFTERCARE OF SHOW STOCK

Tired birds, home again after the heat and scramble of the verage show, need a little extra care. As they are unbasketed, iey should have their heads, feet and legs washed with a ɔlution of some safe disinfectant as sold for personal use. ᴐettol is excellent. Dried off with a towel, the birds are then aced in the same pens from which they were taken in the iorning.

A feed of some easily digested but nourishing food is given.

Bread and milk is excellent and prevents birds, which may have become unduly thirsty, from gorging with water. It also fills out crops very quickly and birds rest awhile after such a feed.

Provided there is nothing untoward the next morning (no suspicious sneezing, for instance) each bird should be taken from the penning room and placed in a cockerel box. The airier, cooler conditions will tone them up and enable the birds to be brought back to maximum condition in time for the next show.

Because they are already trained and docile, exhibits will not need to be brought back to the penning room until two or three days before the next show. Just in time for them to be washed (if necessary) or worked on by their owner before their next outing.

Aftercare includes keeping a watchful eye on the beak and toenails to see that they do not become unduly long. This can happen when poultry spend too much time penned up and not enough running free.

Likeliest troubles deriving directly from conditions attached to showing are as under:

1. *Overgrown spurs*

Adult males of soft-feathered breeds may grow long, harsh spurs which detract from appearance and can cause infertility when the birds are put down to breed. These should be shortened.

A piece of thick cloth, such as flannel, is soaked in cold water. It is pushed down so that the spur protrudes but the shank is protected by the material. An old table knife is heated until the blade is red-hot. The spur is then removed at appropriate length by using the blade with a sawing motion. There is no bleeding since the wound is cauterized as it is formed.

Game fowl always retain their natural spurs.

2. *Bumble foot and corns*

Birds of heavy build, both large and bantam, may get bumble foot or corns as they grow older and are frequently occupying cockerel boxes where there is little room for a bird to flutter down from its perch, and litter is sparse on the floor. In bumble foot there is an abscess under the pad of the foot, causing lameness, with a hard corn at its centre. The foot should be soaked in warm water containing disinfectant. When the skin is clean and soft the swelling should be lanced and pus expressed, the corn being lifted out. The resultant hole should be plugged with cottonwool soaked in disinfectant solution and the bird kept in a small pen with copious amounts of soft litter until it recovers. Treatment of a corn, without the attendant abscess, is similar.

### 3. Crop troubles

If a bird has been unfortunate enough to receive some unsuitable food in its pen (from some otherwise well intentioned person) at a show, it may have a slight degree of sourcrop on return. This will be indicated by the crop holding fluid, due to excessive drinking, droppings being watery and evil smelling.

A weak solution of bicarbonate of soda (or some proprietary indigestion mixture) should be given via the beak. After gently massaging the crop the bird should be left for about a quarter of an hour. It is then held by the legs with its head hanging down while the crop is gently and persistently massaged and the contents emptied into a container which can be disposed of. The fluid which comes away will be extremely smelly.

The bird can usefully be without food and water for a few hours and then be given bread and milk, without cod liver oil or sugar being added. It is carefully examined at next feeding time. If there is again distention and fluid, the process should be repeated. Staple diet should be bread and milk until the condition clears up, when normal food can be given.

# INDEX

Ancona, 66
  compared with Leghorn, 84
  run size required, 6
Andalusian, 66
  compared with Minorca, 85
Arks, 13
Australorps, 70
  common faults, 76

Bantams, 67 - 8
  feed, 37
  ornamental, 77 - 8
Barbu d'Anvers, 67
Barbu d'Uccle, 67
Barley, 30
Barnevelder, 65, 66
Barred Rocks, common fault, 76
Bathing, 60 - 2
Bodies, faults, 80, 81
Brahma, 66
  compared with Cochin, 88
Bread and milk, for conditioning, 53 - 4
Breeders, 2 - 3
Breeding stock
  double-mating, 41
  feeding, 45 - 6
  of experienced breeders, 42
  qualities required, 39 - 40
  recommended relationships, 44
  selection, 39 - 42
  two-pen system, 45
Breeds
  classification, 65 - 8
  effect on management pattern, 33
  similarities, 78 - 9, 84 - 91
British Poultry Standards, 64
Broody breakers, 26
Buckwheat, 31
Buff Rocks, common faults, 76
Bullying, 47
Bumble foot, 96

Campine, 66
Canary seed, 31
  for conditioning, 53
Carbohydrates, 30
Cochin, compared with Brahma, 88
Cockerel boxes, 25, 47
Cockerels, rearing, 48
Cod liver oil, 31
  during conditioning, 53
Colour breeds, 65 - 7

Concrete
  buildings, 21
  constituents, 17 - 18
  making slabs and posts, 20 - 1
  path-laying method, 19 - 20
  quantities required, 18
Conditioning
  stages, 50

Dari, 31
Detergents, 63
Digestive problems, 97
Dorkings
  common faults, 76
  compared with Sussex, 86
Double-mating, 41
Draughtproofing, 15
Dressing plumage, 56
  see also Head dressing
Dropping boards, 16
Drying birds, 62
  home-made boxes, 63
Duck foot, 78

Earlobes, white, 48, 56 - 8
Exercise, 25
  for breeding stock, 45
Exhibitors
  breeders/exhibitors, 2
  characteristics, 1
  foundation stock breeders, 2 - 3
  leading, 1 - 2

Fats, 31
Faverolle, carriage of tail, 53
Feathers, see Plumage
Feed
  after shows, 95 - 6
  alternative methods, 29 - 30
  at maturity, 37
  balancing the diet, 31 - 2
  categories, 30 - 1
  during rearing, 49
  for breeding stock, 45 - 6
  for conditioning, 53 - 4
  for hard feather birds, 37
  from eight weeks old, 34 - 5
  from twelve weeks old, 35 - 6
  home-made mashes, 29
    examples, 32 - 3
  importance of allowing adequate time, .
  importance of palatability, 33

102

104